LEADERSHIP AND PRODUCTIVITY

Chandler Publications in

ANTHROPOLOGY AND SOCIOLOGY

LEONARD BROOM, *Editor*

LEADERSHIP *and*

PRODUCTIVITY

Some Facts of Industrial Life

ROBERT DUBIN
Research Professor of Sociology
UNIVERSITY OF OREGON

GEORGE C. HOMANS
Professor of Social Relations
HARVARD UNIVERSITY

FLOYD C. MANN
Program Director, Survey Research Center
Professor of Psychology
UNIVERSITY OF MICHIGAN

DELBERT C. MILLER
Professor of Sociology and Business Administration
INDIANA UNIVERSITY

 **CHANDLER PUBLISHING COMPANY**
An Intext Publisher   •   Scranton, Pennsylvania 18515

Contents

Preface

What is known about leadership and supervision as they influence productivity? This volume assembles most of the strands of empirical knowledge and combines these with the more viable sociological theories of human effort and cooperation. The book focuses on what actually transpires in man-leader relations. The analysis of leadership also probes the core of the "organization man" issue on which contemporary attention fixes: whether man shall master organizations or become their creature. We authors are sensitive to the essential humanity of men, but do not assume that men are exploited when led, or manipulated as puppets when supervised. Interestingly enough, we find that the organization's representative closest to the worker, his supervisor, is master neither of his own role nor of his subordinates' output.

This book addresses the broad question: "What are the social systems in which supervisors and workers interact to produce the goods and services of society?" The immediate question is: "Can leaders and supervisors really influence their associates and followers to increase productivity in their common enterprise?" Thus the book attacks an intensely practical problem and contains significant original contributions to knowledge about supervisory influences on productivity as well as other consequences of supervisory practices for the behaviors of subordinates. Each analysis is made in the framework of formal organizations and thereby contributes to the recently recognized field called organization theory.

There is a minimum of ideology mixed with the analysis. This feature is especially notable in a field of inquiry which has had ideology as a central component of much theorizing. Each author is committed to important ideas in his personal beliefs—for example, we are sympathetic to the idea that democratic administration is a desirable goal, whose partial attainment may only maximize a democratic atmosphere itself. Yet none of us bends facts to fit an ideological position, nor do we ignore facts that might weaken a personally preferred conclusion.

All of us emphasize technology as an important influence on productivity and supervisory practices. Each, in his chapter, attempts to advance knowledge about the human-relations dimension of supervision by showing some of the subtle and sophisticated linkages between leaders and followers. Finally, organizational variables play a prominent role in each of our analyses.

We employ a diversity of strategies. Dubin and Mann have emphasized inductive conclusions from empirical data. Both also reconstruct theory in order to cover facts not within the scope of old theory. Homans's analytical strategy is to employ models of human behavior found viable in other settings to make sense out of industrial behavior. This approach limits attention only to certain kinds of empirical data adequate to test the specific predictions of his theoretical models. Miller adopts a historical approach in which the moving equilibrium of industrial organizations, responding to technological and other innovations, is shown to create conflicting demands upon the foreman.

In spite of the diverse analytical approaches, the conclusions reached are largely consistent with each other. When different approaches converge on similar conclusions, they take on added plausibility. Even so, we want to emphasize that we do not have final answers. We do have faith, however, that better answers to practical problems of supervision may come out of a funding of knowledge such as is represented by this volume.

To look at reality in order that it may be improved by human design requires a special orientation to the world of affairs.

Many academicians relate to industry as consultants whose impulse is to have definite answers for problems encountered. In the nature of consultantship there is a tendency to ignore what is not known and try to make do with what is known. The consultant, like the medical doctor, must write his prescriptions from the list of known and available medicines. But each of us—though we have all been consultants to industry and hope we have benefited our clients—is in the science business primarily, not in the consulting profession. We have always demanded a feedback from our sorties into industry: new facts and insights gained where the work of society is done. We hope these pages make this knowledge available.

ROBERT DUBIN

LEADERSHIP AND PRODUCTIVITY

1

Supervision and Productivity: Empirical Findings and Theoretical Considerations

ROBERT DUBIN

The purpose of this chapter is to draw together the empirical studies of supervision as it affects productivity. The question is: What difference does the style or quality of supervision make for the productivity of those being supervised?

SOME VIEWPOINTS

The question asked is a simple one. In the past it has evoked simple answers.

The proponents of *scientific management* have demonstrated that work simplification and rationalization improves productivity. Insofar as the supervisor simplifies and rationalizes the work of his subordinates, he presumably affects their output favorably.

The exponents of *welfare capitalism* concluded that humane treatment of subordinates improves their devotion to the organization employing them, and that this increased commitment conduces to higher output. This theme finds its contemporary echo in the welfare-state view of workers and the conditions of their well-being under which they increase work effort on behalf of the enterprise. The supervisor presumably is a key figure in according humane treatment to subordinates and is therefore crucial in building and sustaining high-level productivity.

At a more advanced stage of capitalism, it has been urged by devotees of *group dynamics* that participation in decisions about their own welfare and working circumstances enhances commitment, and through that enhancement, the productivity of subordinates. The *socialist theory* of worker motivation reaches the same substantial conclusion that participation—representative participation—in the management of an industrial enterprise increases commitment to the collective undertaking, and by this means also increases productivity. Clearly, in both of these views, the most immediate point of decision sharing with subordinates is in the daily contact with supervisors so that the supervisor is one key figure in the productivity equation.

Employing a model of economic man, *incentive systems* are designed under capitalism and socialism to pay off workers in accordance with their output, on the assumption that worker self-interest in the value of the payoff overrides all other considerations. In the effort to maximize payoff the worker will monitor his own efforts to achieve high output levels in seeking high-level payoffs. The industrial rate-buster and the Stakhanovite socialist worker are archetypical economic men. But even economic man needs some supervison, at least to have constantly called to his attention the still-to-be-attained payoffs available. Thus, supervision does play a role in keeping attention focused upon the payoff rewards of individual effort and productivity.

Each of the major orientations just reviewed concerning the functions of supervisors in affecting productivity derives from a theory of organization. However the linkage between the individual worker and his work organization is formulated, a supervisor mediates the linkage. The supervisor is a leader of an organized group in an organization whose efforts are directed toward achieving organizational goals.

ORGANIZATION THEORY

The most general conclusion of this chapter's analysis is that productive supervisory practices are those appropriate to the organization in which the supervisor functions. Different kinds of supervisory behaviors are effective because they are suited to special kinds of organizations.

Students of industrial behavior have taken a long time to reach the pedestrian conclusion that many different styles of supervision are effective. Analyses of the management of scientists in industry make clear that the supervisory style appropriate to the direction of their work is different from foreman behavior on the automobile-assembly line.[1] From the study of coal mining has come the understanding that when the technology of mining is radically changed supervisory behaviors appropriate to the new technology differ markedly from those in established traditions.[2] Supervision that is effective with bank employees contrasts with that which is successful with sales crews.[3] Actual studies of working behaviors have sampled a fair number of work settings and have revealed significant variety in the successful supervisory practices found among them.

---

[1] For studies of scientists in industry see William Kornhauser, *Scientists in Industry: Conflict and Accommodation* (Berkeley: University of California Press, 1962), and Simon Marcson, *The Scientist in American Industry* (Princeton: Industrial Relations Section, Princeton University, 1958). Foreman behavior on the automobile-assembly line is sketched out in Charles R. Walker, Robert H. Guest, and Arthur N. Turner, *The Foreman on the Assembly Line* (Cambridge, Mass.: Harvard University Press, 1956).

[2] As well described in E. L. Trist and K. W. Bansforth, "Some Social and Psychological Consequences of the Longwall Method of Coal Getting," *Human Relations*, 4:3-38 (December 1951).

[3] For a study of bank employees see: Chris Argyris, *Organization of a Bank* (New Haven: Yale Labor and Management Center, 1954), while an excellent study of supervision of sales crews is G. F. F. Lombard, *Behavior in a Selling Group: A Case Study of Interpersonal Relations in a Department Store* (Boston: Harvard Business School, Division of Research, 1955).

The growing body of evidence speaks loudly for the idea that in the supervision of industrial and commercial work highly varied practices prove successful in given work settings. Nevertheless, students of industry and industrial administrators still seek a "one best method" of supervision much as the originators of scientific management and work rationalization were captivated by the hope that individual work tasks could be standardized in a "one best method."

This chapter is not the place for an examination into the reasons for the lag in thinking about supervisors. It is sufficient to point out that much theorizing about industrial supervision assumes its unitary character and prescribes behaviors on the basis of that assumption.

The alternative assumption is that supervision is an integral part of an organization in operation. Whatever characteristics the organization may have will influence the styles of supervision that are appropriate. Supervision is an integral part of a functioning organization and inevitably reflects the features that make types of organizations unique.

The designation "organization" is not limited to the unit commonly called a company or a business firm. For example, the research unit of a company is an organization since it has features that clearly distinguish it from the production shop or the sales force. Furthermore, this research division requires a system of supervision different from that of the shop or sales organization. An organization, then, is any distinctive unit, the features of which (perhaps technology, operating conditions, product, size, location) influence human relations in it.

In this discussion, particular attention will be focused on those human relations involving interaction of supervisors with subordinates. The central analytical problem is this: how to sort out the influences of supervisory behavior from other influences that play upon productivity.

Two general possibilities present themselves. (1) On the assumption that supervision accounts for a fixed and sizeable proportion of the variation in output, comparisons may be made between different kinds of supervision to see which has the highest positive correlation with productivity. This has been the strategy followed in most studies of supervision.[4] (2) An alternative approach is to ask under what circumstances does supervision make more or less difference than do *other factors* affecting productivity? There may very well be considerable variability in the *relative* importance of supervision from one organizational setting to another.

Why bother to distinguish these two approaches? The answer is very simple. Suppose that supervision in a given situation affects only 10 per cent of output, all other factors accounting for the other 90 per cent. Suppose studies permitted management to increase the effectiveness of supervision in relation to output from 30 per cent to 60 per cent. The net effect of this doubling of supervisory effectiveness would be to increase productivity by only 3 per cent, since supervision affects only 10 per cent of the total variation in output. A business manager confronted with a situation like this hypothetical one would probably concentrate on many other factors to increase productivity before turning to improve supervision.

This hypothetical illustration makes clear a major difficulty in interpreting studies of supervision and productivity. When an over-all measure of productivity, one that reflects the impact of all factors influencing it, is employed in relation to some one specific measure of supervisory behavior, the correlations usually turn out to be very low, as will be shown in the subsequent analysis. Furthermore, the "best" supervisory practices do not seem to produce very much greater output than the "worst" with which they are compared. These two disappointing results may

---

See, as one among the many references cited in the following discussion, one of the important Ohio State University studies which employed this strategy: E. F. Fleishman, E. F. Harris, and R. D. Burtt, *Leadership and Supervision in Industry* (Columbus: Ohio State University Press, 1955).

obscure a genuine and important impact of supervision *within that range* over which it actually influences productivity. Some of the simultaneous effects of supervision and other factors on productivity will be sorted out in the following analysis of individual studies.

The purposes and functions of supervision are complex and varied. It may influence productivity but it surely influences much more as well. Some of the many products of supervisory styles include subordinates' morale level, their feelings of well-being, their interest in long-time membership in the organization, and their effectiveness in cooperating with each other. Presumably supervision affects these aspects of human relations whether or not each in turn affects productivity. Supervisors also handle technical problems like inspection and quality controls, the repair of technical breakdowns, and work-flow stoppages. The communication channels between management and work force depend upon the supervisor as an essential link, while maintenance of discipline and order usually devolve on the shoulders of the supervisor. Supervisors thus do more than stimulate output and productivity. Indeed, among all the functions of supervisors, the stimulation of individual output *may* be of middling or even minor importance.

That supervisors may perform several functions adds still more complexity to the supervision-productivity relation. Some of these functions may be independent of each other so that the performance of one has no influence on the acceptance by subordinates of the performance of another. On the other hand, the supervisor's performance of two functions may interact upon each other. Thus, a supervisor who shares decisions with subordinates but who is technically incompetent to handle work-flow stoppages may engender a reaction quite different from that toward his colleague who also shares decisions but is technically competent.

In the presence of all these variables, it is necessary to consider a normative problem: What is meant by "best" supervision or "desirable" supervisory practices? These terms usually denote a particular system of supervision having some significant ideological or ethical foundation. The very appeal of the ideology ("democratic leadership") or the ethics ("individual self-realization") makes any questioning of the associated system of supervision appear immoral. If, however, evidence rather than belief guides the evaluation of supervisory practices, then a negative conclusion should not be interpreted as an attack on morals, nor a positive conclusion be considered in favor of moral values.

CULTURE, SUPERVISION, AND PRODUCTIVITY

The most general view of productivity and supervision relates them to a society or culture. It is essential to ask: "Do the characteristic structures and features of a culture influence modes of production in it as well as the supervision of productive activities?"

Societies and cultures are described by such terms as pastoral, nomadic, preindustrial, and industrial, suggesting that a central feature of any culture is the mode of earning a living and supporting the populace. The anthropological viewpoint gives heavy emphasis to cultural determinism of working and productive behaviors by its attention to (1) the kinds of pursuits that engage human energies for the production of goods and services, and (2) the particular working behaviors that produce the goods and services. Working behaviors in a society are determined by the culture which characterizes that society. Supervisory patterns in the work arena are often determined by cultural features (as by a kinship system which has additional functions).

In the modern urban-industrial society, culture also makes a difference. The interuniversity studies of comparative national industrial systems[5] illustrate that management and supervision are culturally defined. For example, a managerial system may

---

[5] One of the volumes in this series that is especially pertinent to this point is Frederick H. Harbison and Charles A. Myers, *Management in the Industrial World* (New York: McGraw-Hill Book Company, 1959).

be grounded in family ownership of enterprises and accordingly display nepotism in recruitment of managers, as in portions of Italian industry. The efficiency of supervision under family nepotism rests partly on the manager's loyalty to the owners of the enterprise. But at the same time, the knowledge that promotion opportunities are limited influences the responses of rank-and-file workers to supervisory practices.

Over the long run there may be a tendency to develop a universal system of management adequate to the demands of high-precision technology. In the short run, however, it seems that culture leaves its unmistakable impress on the characteristic modes of managing the enterprise. For example, Harbison and Burgess[6] show that substantially similar types of steel industries in West Germany and the United States had different managerial structures with much higher proportions of middle managers in the American establishments than in their German counterparts. Technological differences do not account for such difference between German and American management structures. German management, being centralized at the top, may reflect the characteristic centralization of decision making in German government and culture. The technological emphasis and professionalization of industrial occupations in American society finds its expression in a higher proportion of staff people to all managers, and a bulging of the middle management ranks in American industry.

The impact of culture is even clearer in the contrast between productive enterprises under communism and capitalism. The structures of management in an American factory and in a Soviet factory comparable in technology are markedly different. Some of the Soviet agencies of control are absent in Western industry. Correspondingly, some of the controls of capitalist production are not to be found under Communism.[7]

[6] Frederick H. Harbison and Eugene W. Burgess, "Modern Management in Western Europe," *American Journal of Sociology*, 60:15-23 (1954).

The impact of culture may also be observed in colonial nations undergoing industrialization. Their industries are typically
staffed in the middle and higher reaches of management, in
some instances in the entire ranks of management, by technically competent foreigners. Binationalism in industry, with natives
in the ranks of workers and foreigners in most or all of management, builds into the productive situation many real or potential
antagonisms that may mitigate against high productivity even
though the requisite technology is available.[8]

Many characteristics of a culture influence industrial supervision and productivity. Cultural relativity makes it important to judge industrial effectiveness or efficiency *inside* a system
rather than among national systems. Varied structures and
modes of supervision reflect special cultural features. These are
surely among the great sources of differences in productivity
among nations and even among regions within nations. An understanding of cultural relativity provides an important corrective for faulty generalization about the "one best supervisory structure" or the most effective supervisory practices for a given industry or especially for an entire industrial complex. It is obviously necessary under these circumstances, to be cautious in
reaching global generalizations like the following declaration by
Likert, one of the spokesmen for the "new management" and a
leader in survey research on industrial behavior:

. . . the general conclusion proposed here appears to make the modi-
fied theory of management widely applicable not only within the

---

[7] For an early analysis of industrial controls in Soviet industry see
Alexander Vucinich, "The Structure of Factory Control in the Soviet
Union," *American Sociological Review*, 15:179-186 (April 1950). This
may be contrasted with Peter Drucker's treatment of control in the
General Motors Corporation: *Concept of the Corporation* (New York:
John Day Co., 1946), especially pages 63-71.

[8] In this connection see Everett C. Hughes, "Queries Concerning
Industry and Society Growing Out of Study of Ethnic Relations in
Industry," *American Sociological Review*, 14:211-220 (April 1949).

United States but to the management problems of any organization in any nation or society. Extensive research will be needed to test this statement, but it appears to be valid and illustrates the manner in which the general conclusion may broaden widely the applicability of fundamental principles.[9]

The industrial world is composed of many national sectors and regional divisions, each characterized by special cultural features and levels of development. Among them, the structures of management and the modes of work supervision manifest corresponding diversity.

TECHNOLOGY, SUPERVISION, AND PRODUCTIVITY

The most notable consequence of advances in technology, as Homans amplifies in the next chapter, is that man-hour productivity increases with transfer of labor operations from men to machines. In the United States, for example, over-all man-hour productivity has risen about 3 per cent per year, at least since World War I, and probably had increased at an even higher annual rate from the turn of the century until then. Increases in man-hour productivity have been largely the consequence of the efficiency built into machines, a major fact to keep in mind when considering productivity and the influences that bear upon it.

TECHNOLOGY AND MANAGEMENT STRUCTURE

Only recently has there been reborn an interest in the core feature of the modern industrial world—the technologies upon which it is grounded. Social scientists and management theorists have been preoccupied for several decades with "human problems" and human relations in work organizations. A recent analysis could discover fewer than three dozen research studies

---

[9] Rensis Likert, "Effective Supervision: An Adaptive and Relative Process," *Personnel Psychology*, 11:317-332 (1958), quoted from p. 328.

in the American, British, French, and German literature empirically dealing with social aspects of the man-machine relationship.[10] This paucity is a harsh commentary on the neglect of
technology during the current preoccupation with the psyche
of man in industry.

The idea that special technologies have associated with
them variations in the structure and function of management is
a recent notion that has challenged traditional managerial thinking. Research by Joan Woodward[11] on British industry has emphasized the importance of technology in structuring management. Woodward's small monograph, *Management and Technology,* has precipitated lively controversy since its publication in
1958.

Woodward classified approximately 100 English firms according to a simple feature of the technology characterizing
their production. She distinguished (1) those firms that produced goods in small batches or in units, from (2) the large-batch
and mass-production firms, and both of these from (3) companies employing continuous-process production. Among the 24
small-batch and unit-production firms, she found that the median number of levels of management authority was only 3, with
a range from 2 to 4 (see Figure 1). Among the 31 mass-production firms, the median number of levels of management authority was 4; the range was from 3 to 8 or more, with 13 of the 31
firms having 5 or more levels of authority as contrasted with none
among the unit-production firms. In the 25 companies employing continuous-process technologies, the median number of levels of management was 6, with but 2 firms having only 4 levels
of authority; the rest had 5 or more, and 10 had 7 or more.

Thus, on the simple feature of levels of authority in the

_____

[10] See the study by Martin Meissner, "Behavioral Adaptations to Industrial Technology" (unpublished Ph.D. dissertation, Dept. of
Sociology, University of Oregon, 1963).

[11] Joan Woodward, *Management and Technology* (London: Her
Majesty's Stationery Office, 1958).

firm, it became clear that the production technology was a determinant of managerial structure. Technology made a difference in the structure of management in spite of a high level of communication between and among the managerial groups in Great Britain, and certainly in the South East Essex area where the study was made. Furthermore, British management practice has been strongly influenced by British management theorists, particularly Lyndall Urwick, which could result in great similar-

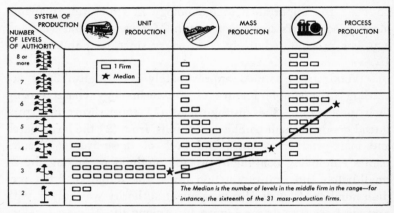

Figure 1. The Number of Levels in Management Hierarchy. (Used by permission from Joan Woodward, *Management and Technology,* cited in footnote 11.)

ities in the structure of management in spite of technological differences among the companies. The fact that there is such marked technological impact on the structure of management leads one to believe that the technology of an industry is an essential influence structuring management and also, at least by inference, the functions and character of supervision.

A closer look at the system of supervision in terms of span of control and ratio of managers and supervisors to workers likewise reveals the technological factor dominant. Woodward found that for the unit-production companies, the median span of control (number of persons controlled) by first-line supervision was between 21 and 30. The median span rose to between 41 and 50 in mass-production industries. In process-production companies, however, the median span of control of first-line supervisors was lowest, between 11 and 20 workers. Furthermore, the distribution of companies according to their span of control, for each type of technology, was characteristically different as shown in Figure 2.

SYSTEM OF PRODUCTION / NUMBER OF PERSONS CONTROLLED	UNIT PRODUCTION	MASS PRODUCTION	PROCESS PRODUCTION
Unclassified	□	□	
81-90		□ □	□ I Firm ★ Median
71-80		□	
61-70		□ □ □ □ □	
51-60	□	□ □ □ □	
41-50	□ □ □	□ □ □ □ □ □ □ □ □ ★	
31-40	□ □ □	□ □ □ □ □	□
21-30	□ □ □ □ □ ★	□	□ □ □ □ □ □
11-20	□ □ □ □ □	□	□ □ □ □ □ □ ★
10 or less	□		□ □ □ □ □ □

Figure 2. Span of Control in First-Line Supervision. (Used by permission from Joan Woodward, *Management and Technology*, cited in footnote 11.)

Turning to the ratio of managers and supervisors to other personnel, the impact of technology is also significant, as revealed in Figure 3. The ratio of managers and supervisory staff to other personnel is lowest in unit-production and highest in continuous-process industries, with mass-production industries falling in between. The differences are very sharp. In continuous-process production the ratio of managers and supervisors to other personnel is between 1 to 7 and 1 to 8, whereas in unit production the ratio ranges from 1 to 24 to as low as 1 to 49. In mass production, the ratio ranges from 1 to 14 through 1 to 18.

It should be noted that the ratio of management personnel to workers is little affected by size of firm for mass-production and continuous-process technologies. With a unit-production technology there are more workers per supervisor for firms with about 1000 employees than for either smaller or larger firms, but regardless of company size, fewer managers and supervisors are required for unit-production technologies than for mass-produc-

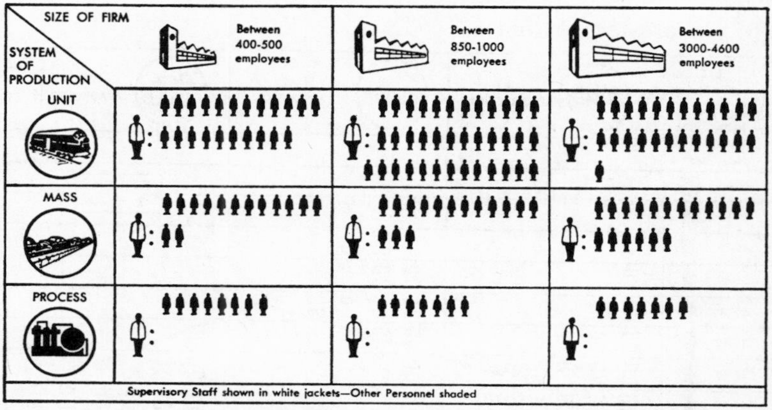

Figure 3. The Ratio of Managers and Staff to Other Personnel. (Used by permission from Joan Woodward, *Management and Technology,* cited in footnote 11.)

tion or continuous-process technologies. The simple measure of the ratio of managers and supervisors to other personnel is clearly related to the technology employed in the industry and is relatively little influenced by the size of the firm.

TECHNOLOGY AND RESPONSIBILITY

Some implications of the impact of technology on the location of responsibility for production are interesting to examine. In continuous-process industries like oil and gas manufacture, the high ratio of managers and supervisors to other personnel is probably a consequence of: (1) the potentiality of an error causing substantial loss in the process should it go on unattended and unnoticed, and (2) the resultant concentration in the ranks of managers and supervisors of inspection and control functions with respect to the technological process. Thus, with high-speed and continuous-process technologies the direct control of technology itself is transferred from operatives to management. (A similar transfer is characteristic of data-processing operations, where control of machines becomes critical, especially in programing the machines, and many of the control and surveillance functions in monitoring quality and quantity of output are transferred from worker level to management.)

As technology in the future tends toward continuous-process manufacture, there will be a shift of control of product quality and quantity from workers to supervisory and managerial personnel. The supervisor will become more immediately involved in the control of output than he is at present. The manager of the machine in continuous-process technologies is no longer primarily the supervisor of people but rather the supervisor of the technology.

On the other hand, in unit production where the time dimension for the production of the unit of output is relatively long, and where the individual is likely to be involved in the production of substantial subassemblies or of the entire product, the control of actual output and quality can be maintained at the worker-operator level. Relatively high levels of skills may be required at the worker level, skills including not only the technical performance of work operations, but also some knowledge about correction of operating errors, inspection, and control. Where the control functions reside in the hands of the worker, the need for supervision is reduced. Woodward's study confirms the consequence, which is a low ratio of managers and supervisors to workers.

The analog to worker-centered responsibility is to be found in the industrial research laboratory, where typically there is unit production (the individual research project), and where there is "colleague authority" in Marcson's sense.[12] Col-

---

[12] Simon Marcson, *op. cit.* in note 1.

league authority means reference to peers rather than to re-search managers of problems requiring decision. Much is made in the supervision of research activities of the need for maximizing colleague authority and the individual scientist's control of quantity and quality of production. The fact is, however, as Woodward's data show, that the opportunity for fixing production responsibility at the worker level exists alike in manual operations and in scientific and intellectual operations, providing the manual operations involve *unit-production technologies*.[13] The supervisory problems of maintaining quantity and quality of output are the same for highly technical people in research and development activities and for workers in unit-production industrial operations.

TECHNOLOGY AND MANAGERIAL COSTS

There are several secondary productivity consequences of variations in supervisory staffing in relation to technology. The simple per worker costs of supervision are considerably less in unit production than in continuous-process production, with mass production midway position between these two. Insofar as management is counted as an indirect cost of production, unit-production systems save money, all other things being equal.

Commitment to the organization on the part of workers and the skill necessary to make the commitment effective in high-quality work vary with the nature of technology. In continuous-process production, commitment may be minimal since supervisors and managers assume the burden of being sure the technological processes are performed adequately. Commitment must presumably be much higher in unit production, since those same responsibilities devolve directly on the worker.

Considerable "cost" may be impressed into the production

---

[13] A recent popular article by Vance Packard described two instances where worker-centered responsibility was effective, and in both cases a unit-production technology was employed. See "A Chance for Everyone to Grow," *Reader's Digest*, 83:114-118 (November 1963).

process if inappropriate supervisory styles are applied under given technological conditions. If close supervision is used in unit production, it may fail or be inefficient. "Democratic" supervision in continuous-process production may prove extremely costly where errors are made in the process operations.

Another way of looking at one of the consequences of the impact of technology on supervision is to note that unit-production technologies have the most "flat" managerial structure and also the fewest managers and supervisors in relation to other personnel. Thus, the total number of managers and the complexity of the managerial structure are both minimal in unit production. On the other extreme, in process production, the number of authority levels in management is highest and the ratio of managers and supervisors to other personnel is also highest. In going from unit production to continuous-process production (mass production lying between unit and continuous production) there is a shift toward the total management component in staffing the enterprise, with more levels of managers and more managers per worker. Management of managers and supervisors, as distinct from management of workers, becomes a critical problem in continuous-process industries. In the area of managing managers we have minimal knowledge and a great deal of speculation.[14]

There is a high probability that it will become increasingly difficult to view the costs of management as "overhead" or "indirect" in continuous-process technologies because so much of the total manpower investment will be in the managerial component. Managers carry relatively high unit prices. The sheer size of the managerial payroll will surely have an impact on production-cost analyses and may bring the development of new ideas regarding the costliness of managers in production.

In passing, mention may be made of other organizational

---

[14] One of the early students of this problem was Melville Dalton. See his "Managing the Managers," *Human Organization*, 14:4-10 (1955).

variables that affect complexity of managerial structure. Organizational centralization and decentralization and the structures that flow from them also produce variations in supervisory practices. The technological variable is not the only one that affects managerial practices, and, either directly or indirectly, the productivity of workers.

SUPERVISORS AND GROUP ATMOSPHERES

The question put at the beginning of this chapter implies: What atmospheres created by supervisors affect productivity of their subordinates?

This problem has been approached polemically and with relatively inadequate research. It is useful to begin with a statement of one view of the supervisor's role in creating a working-group atmosphere.

Maier[15] observed: "We are entering a period in work relations where mental cruelty is becoming an appropriate charge in a grievance committee meeting as it is in the divorce court."[16] Specifically, self-determination of behavior is more acceptable than determination by others: "It is apparent that a person accepts his own decisions more often than he does another's. Group decisions are more readily accepted, but may sacrifice quality."[17] Nevertheless: "When production is a matter of coordination of group activity, it can be increased by stimulating the group to decide on a goal. In such cases the goal set should be unanimously approved . . . Group decision thus becomes an extremely important factor in determining the performance of a team of workers."[18]

Maier's thinking starts with the mental well-being or psychic comfort of the worker and concludes that somehow or other this is positively related to production. The argument is a very

---

[15] Norman R. F. Maier, *Psychology in Industry* (Boston: Houghton Mifflin Company, 1955) (2nd ed.).

[16] *Ibid.*, p. 137.   [17] *Ibid.*, p. 141.   [18] *Ibid.*, pp. 151- 152.

tenuous one and it may be accurate. However, the evidence is meager and when marshaled gives weak support to the conclusion. Participation in decisions about own behavior does not necessarily lead to maximizing own behavior to achieve organizational objectives, with a payoff in mental comfort. Even the evidence of the quality of group decisions calls into serious doubt the effectiveness of groups in making production decisions. For example, the original work by Taylor[19] made clear that even in the number of ideas produced in group discourse while "brainstorming" the group output was measurably less than individual output under similar circumstances.

Drucker[20] has pointed out that the trend in modern industrial work emphasizes individual jobs as well as group or team jobs. He noted that many maintenance jobs are individual jobs and that these will increase in number with increasing automation of industry. Furthermore, many sales jobs are individual jobs, and these will also increase in number as secondary economic activity provides an increasing proportion of employment opportunities. An important corrective to current emphasis on the "groupness" of industrial work is to realize that there are now and will probably be an increasing proportion of all jobs which will *not* be performed in groups but will be performed individually and outside of group contexts. For individual jobs, the group theory of motivation simply will not apply and new studies will be necessary to find out how the lone worker can be moved to a high level of productivity and sustained there as a member of a modern work organization. This area is one of present ignorance among industrial psychologists and sociologists as well as among management practitioners.

---

[19] D. W. Taylor, P. C. Berry, and C. H. Block, "Does Group Participation When Using Brainstorming Facilitate or Inhibit Creative Thinking," *Administrative Science Quarterly*, 3:23-47 (1958).

[20] Peter Drucker, *The Practice of Management* (New York: Harper and Bros., 1954).

SUPERIOR-SUBORDINATE INTERACTION

A more analytical reading of the group-dynamics literature was presented by Arensberg and Tootel, who drew the following conclusions:

But the Mayoites seem to have misread their own data. Reanalysis shows that their "teamwork" and "informal organization" are less multifactorial results, or even steady states, than emergent results of prior and continuous managerial and flow-of-work changes. The process took the form of this definite order of development: (1) an increase of managerial initiative, (2) followed by an increase of inter-worker communication, (3) followed by an increase of redressive up-the-line action of the worker upon foreman or spokesman, (4) which resulted in further changes of rewarding sorts in managerial actions, (5) changing individual attitudes, (6) reaching expression as new group attitudes or morale (the "norms" of Homans), (7) which won informal sanction by the workers on one another, (8) and stimulated further releases of individual output and productivity.[21]

Arensberg and Tootel go on to state: "It is worthwhile reiterating the discovery of the 'interactionists' that this process, and the gain in productivity it brings about, seems to have *very delicate and narrow limits*."[22] Their summary is worthy of note:

Indeed, present evidence suggests that the release of productivity is not so much limited by human capacity or by "diminishing returns" of maximization, as older efficiency doctrines have it, as it is dependent upon some "feedback" between worker initiative and managerial facilitation. The next advance in our understanding will come when we work out the empirical characteristics of this process.[23]

At a later point in their paper, Arensberg and Tootel conclude with:

---

[21] Conrad M. Arensberg and Geoffrey Tootel, "Plant Sociology: Real Discoveries and New Problems," in Mirra Komarovsky (ed.) *Common Frontiers in the Social Sciences* (Glencoe: Free Press, 1957), p. 316.

[22] *Ibid.*   [23] *Ibid.*, p. 317.

. . . the finding that the process of the social release of productivity, in the empirical studies so far made, is not a matter of offering rewards alone. . . . We must remember that a plant is not only a place of performance tests and output scores. It is a power situation where a lesser-powered group is performing a test imposed and surveyed by a higher. Even if the management with consummate skill were to use all the goals of its employees there is both theoretical and empirical reason to doubt that the human "contented cows" stay contented under continuous driving. A "strain" is likely to develop. . . . If, however, for any reason the cumulative process of change . . . which we are discussing, gets under way, a different outcome may ensue. In that case, such a process might move the relevant social system comprising the two groups *toward* some "fusion" so that a common system of shared values might develop about the performance in question.[24]

The statement starts with "the release of productivity" and ends with a "common system of shared values." These are two different things. It still remains to be proved that the shared values are always or ever goals apropos of productivity. This distinction has been recognized by Bakke in his discussion of the "fusion process."[25]

SHARED GOALS

Perhaps the best single piece of empirical evidence bearing on the issue of a shared goal as the stimulus to high-level group effort is found in the celebrated "Robbers Cave Experiment."[26] Two groups of boys in a boy's camp achieved fusion in the solution of a common problem, after they had been deliberately placed in antagonism to each other, only when they realized that the continuous flow of behavior in each group de-

[24] *Ibid.*, p. 332.

[25] E. Wight Bakke, *The Fusion Process* (New Haven: Yale Labor and Management Center, 1953).

[26] Muzafer Sherif, *Intergroup Conflict and Cooperation: The Robbers Cave Experiment* (Norman, Okla.: University Book Exchange, 1961).

pended on overcoming this mutual problem. The groups were driven into each other's arms and into cooperation by the need jointly to solve a problem bigger than each could handle separately. Thus, fusion was achieved between two antagonistic groups in overcoming a common obstacle.

It is worth emphasizing that there is a difference between (1) maintaining steady states in a social system and (2) the reaction of the social system to blockages or obstacles against the normal flow of activities. Empirical evidence does indicate that "fusion" can develop among diverse groups in overcoming obstacles that they face in common. Such evidence appears in Sherif's studies and in the earlier studies of Kurt Lewin, who examined the problems of group decision to achieve eating-habit changes under wartime shortages of food.[27] Sociologists have long called attention to the fact that national unity and social cohesion are usually the products either of acute crises in the social system or of attack from outside. In wars and other major social crises, many intrasocietal differences are set aside in favor of overcoming the obstacles confronting the society as a whole. Fires, floods, and other disasters in industrial establishments automatically override differences between union and management as they work together to overcome the obstacle and restore the plant to productive effectiveness. In a mine disaster, a union and its members, normally struggling against management, may temporarily set aside antagonisms in the common concern to save the men trapped underground. All these instances bear on the fact that "fusion" of groups with different goals can be achieved when they are simultaneously confronted with a common obstacle that halts the normal flow of behavior in the groups.

The maintenance of a steady state like high productivity, and the accompanying values necessary to sustain it, has not been shown to be the product of the "fusion" of diverse goals

[27] Kurt Lewin, *Field Theory in Social Science* (Dorwin Cartwright, ed.) (New York: Harper and Bros., 1951).

and values of the groups involved. Even the neglected and important research of Blake and Mouton[28] has dealt only with problem solving but not with steady-state maintenance.

It is not the purpose here to assert that maintenance of a steady state of high output is impossible, or that it may not be the product of a "fusion" of diverse group values. There is, however, no present empirical evidence to show that the fusion of group values is what sustains steady states in social systems. It is time to devote attention to actual measurement and analysis of this connection.

SUPERVISOR AS ENVIRONMENT FOR WORKERS

One of the direct consequences of Woodward's work was a study by Thurley and Hamblin[29] of five English firms. The purpose of the study was to focus attention on supervisory behaviors that could be directly associated with technological feature of the work. A number of the findings are highly significant for understanding the functions of direct supervision but are beyond the subject matter of this chapter. One technical factor affecting what the supervisor does on his job was the variability of the operations supervised. Supervisors devoted much attention to meeting schedules and to planning sequences of operations as well as to overcoming blockages against continuity of production. In addition, they maintained quality by checking the product rather than the producers. The supervisors also spent significant amounts of time checking machinery—in one department of an electronics company this activity reached 16 per cent of the

---

[28] Some of which is summarized in Robert R. Blake and Jane S. Mouton, "Competition, Communication, and Conformity," and "Conformity, Resistance and Conversion," both in I. A. Berg and B. M. Bass (eds.), *Conformity and Deviation* (New York: Harper and Bros., 1961).

[29] K. E. Thurley and A. C. Hamblin, *The Supervisor and His Job* (London: Her Majesty's Stationery Office, 1963). Comments are based on a prepublication copy of this study.

supervisors' total working time. Dealing with contingencies was another major consumer of supervisors' attention and time.

What is important here is to note that the supervisor is constantly caught up with duties focusing on plans, schedules, machines, and overcoming contingencies that interfere with meeting output expectations. In short, supervisors are supervising technical processes and machines, meeting output standards, and maintaining quality controls. People are relatively incidental and instrumental to these preoccupations, the more so as the technology approaches continuous-flow operations.

Workers, too, perceive this operating system and probably in terms not unlike those of the supervisor. Worker expectations of supervisors are molded just as much as are the behaviors of supervisors by the technical and organizational environment.

Structuring of the supervisor's work responds to technical and organizational imperatives, as will appear in the studies of Fleishman, and consideration for the worker as individual decreases as the technology becomes more complicated and the production schedule demands higher rates of continuous output.

MULTIPLE GOALS OF SUPERVISION

Supervisors are not solely oriented toward building and maintaining the productive level of those supervised. Indeed, as theorists like Maier have indicated, the mental health or psychic well-being of workers may be a coordinate goal of the efforts of supervision, along with productivity. Beside the notion of psychic well-being can be set those of morale, of loyalty, of commitment to organization, as other goals toward which supervisory practices may be directed. These all relate to the connection between employee and organization. In addition, there is an extremely large body of studies and theory dealing with such goals of supervision as maintenance of safety, reduction of employee turnover, minimization of employee grievances, reduction of scrap and other losses, quality control, and plant and equipment maintenance.

It is notable that in pursuit of this incomplete list of goals toward which supervisory behaviors are directed a vast range of activities is to be found, many of which are independent of each other. The supervisor's jobs are many and varied, and it should not be at all surprising to find numerous empirical situations in which the supervisor is little, if at all, concerned with people or with productivity. Certainly, under circumstances of complete machine pacing, for example, the variability in productivity that can be attributed to supervisory practices is probably extremely small.

Morale, feelings of well-being, attitudes toward the company, acceptance or nonacceptance of supervisors, cohesiveness of the work group, employee turnover, or grievance incidence rates are in and of themselves important subjects for study and analysis. Because, however, the major test applied by operating management to any innovations in supervisory practices is the influence these may have on productivity, the authors of studies relating supervisory practices to other outcomes often gratuitously conclude that their results support the belief that productivity will also be positively affected. It is important to keep in mind that the various goals toward which supervisory practices are directed are not necessarily interrelated.

WORKER MORALE AS A GOAL

A number of studies of supervisory behavior concern its influence on morale of workers. Almost invariably the author will conclude that if the supervisor's behavior can raise morale, then there are probably associated increases in productivity. The study may clearly demonstrate that morale does vary according to the behaviors of supervisors, but the conclusion that morale change in turn influences productivity remains unsupported. Indeed, Dubin[30] has pointed out that high morale in a work group may be the basis for successful sabotage of management's productiv-

---

[30] Robert Dubin, *The World of Work* (Englewood Cliffs, N.J.: Prentice-Hall, 1958), especially Chapter 12.

ity goals, and Seashore[31] has shown that high-cohesion work groups may deviate from production norms on *both* the high and the low sides. Since Seashore's data also show that high-cohesion work groups tend to be high-morale groups, his findings support Dubin's conclusion.

As part of the Yale study of automobile assembly-line workers, Turner[32] showed that the attitudes of workers toward the job itself and toward their own foremen were independent. In particular, Turner found that if the job was of primary importance to the workers, then the foreman and his behaviors made relatively little difference in their orientation toward the organization. "It was as if the nature of the job and the nature of supervision, as perceived by workers, were almost separate influences on workers' over-all attitudes."[33]

Kahn, one of the principal investigators in the Michigan researches, concluded the survey of the Michigan studies of supervisors and workers as follows: "None of the major indices of satisfaction (job, supervision, company, etc.) proved either to relate to productivity or to mediate significantly between productivity and such independent variables as role differentiation, delegation, or employee orientation."[34]

Turning directly to evidence on morale, Kahn stated the following:

This research, . . . did not provide positive evidence on the matter of morale in relation of productivity. . . . Indices of worker satisfaction were developed by means of factor analysis, which showed four well-defined dimensions of satisfaction: satisfaction with super-

---

[31] Stanley E. Seashore, *Group Cohesiveness in the Industrial Work Group* (Ann Arbor: Institute for Social Research, University of Michigan, 1954).

[32] Arthur N. Turner, "Foreman, Job, and Company," *Human Relations*, 10:99-112 (1957).

[33] *Ibid.*, p. 111.

[34] Robert L. Kahn, "The Prediction of Productivity," *Journal of Social Issues*, 12:41-49 (1956), p. 44.

vision, with the job itself, with the company as a whole, and with the extrinsic rewards of money, mobility, etc. None of these indices was significantly related to productivity.

In line with a statement already made in this chapter, Kahn stated: "The notion that supervision (among other things) de-

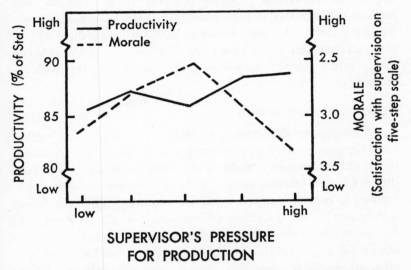

SUPERVISOR'S PRESSURE
FOR PRODUCTION

Figure 4. The Relation of Productivity and Morale to Supervisor's Pressure for Production. (Redrawn from Rensis Likert, "Developing Patterns in Management," cited in footnote 36.)

termines satisfaction, which in turn determines productivity, has been considerably discredited in our eyes."[35]

Likert[36] has presented some other Michigan data which show that productivity increases with supervisor's pressure for more output (Figure 4). Morale also increases up to about the mid range of supervisory pressure for output, after which it de-

---

[35] *Ibid.*, from pp. 46 and 47.

[36] Rensis Likert, "Developing Patterns in Management," in American Management Association, *Strengthening Management for the New Technology* (New York: The Association, 1955).

clines, just as sharply as it increased. Thus, even the data used by one of the strongest exponents of worker autonomy shows that pressure *does* produce more productivity and even increases morale through a portion of the range of increasing supervisory pressure. This observation suggests that social systems respond to leadership pressures in "putting the heat on" and holding subordinates to high expectations. In an organized production situation, workers expect to be asked to produce and be held to reasonable levels of output. Furthermore, if the supervisory pressure is not excessive workers' morale goes up with increasing pressure!

WORKER AUTONOMY AS A GOAL

Management literature is replete with a theme that worker autonomy is a viable goal for supervisory practices. Generally the worker autonomy sought is one best described as the condition wherein workers require little supervision. Sometimes autonomy is specified as the condition requiring minimum "close supervision." The definition of autonomy is almost always in the supervisor-worker context. On its face, worker autonomy should be an acceptable condition for many workers, and it is obviously an aid to supervisors since it reduces their burden.

Kahn,[37] in summarizing the human-relations research program at the University of Michigan, showed that in the studies of clerical and railroad workers the high-productivity groups were supervised in a general fashion rather than in a close or detailed one. This demonstration was the beginning of the repeated emphasis in the Michigan studies, castigating close and detailed supervision and pleading for worker autonomy as one of the important requisites for high output. The idea has persisted to the present and is given renewed emphasis by Likert.[38] But the study of British industry by Argyle, Gardner, and Ciofi[39]

---

[37] Robert L. Kahn, *op. cit.* in note 34.

[38] In his widely acclaimed book, *New Patterns of Management* (New York: McGraw-Hill Book Co., 1961).

[39] Michael Argyle, Godfrey Gardner, and Frank Ciofi, "The Measure-

did not demonstrate autonomy as a central variable in productivity. These data have never been incorporated into the thinking of the Michigan group.

Perhaps these disparate findings can be reconciled by noting that both railroad and clerical workers, the samples from which the Michigan group drew its conclusions, are involved in unit- or batch-production systems. Woodward's studies of technology and management show that the ratio of supervisors to workers is very low in such systems. A correlate of this low ratio, one noted earlier, is that the responsibility of individual workers may be maximal in such systems. A further correlate is that workers in unit-production technologies will produce most when given only general supervision. This relation is to be attributed to the technology rather than to a general principle that all work situations demand maximum autonomy for workers.

The study by Argyle, Gardner, and Ciofi was based on 90 foremen in eight British factories manufacturing electric motors and switchgear. These factories would all probably be classified as employing large-batch or quasi-mass production, with basic technological features different from those in the routine clerical work in a large insurance company and in the railroad gangs studied by the Michigan group. The British study revealed that the only dimension of supervisory behavior which bore a significant relationship to measured output of the departments supervised was punitive or nonpunitive correction by the foreman of worker mistakes and errors. When general supervision was combined with nonpunitive behavior and democratic relations with employees, these three dimensions of supervisor behavior were positively and significantly correlated with output, but together they accounted only for 18 per cent of the variance in output.

Likert reproduced the results of one of his earliest studies

---

ment of Supervisory Methods," *Human Relations*, 10:295-313 (1957) and by the same authors, "Supervisory Methods Related to Productivity, Absenteeism, and Labour Turnover," *Human Relations*, 11:23-40 (1958).

in *New Patterns of Management*[40] in which he compared the difference between superior and mediocre life-insurance agencies. The data show that an attitude of cooperation with his sales agents by the agency manager was found more often among managers of agencies judged superior in performance. The descriptions of the managers were based on agents' evaluations. Furthermore, these same successful managers gave considerably more autonomy to their agents than the less successful managers.

It is not surprising, in view of these results secured when he made one of his first studies of managerial behavior, that Likert would conclude that considerate, nondirective leadership characteristics symbolize modern industrial statesmanship. However, it is obvious that selling life insurance is a classical unit-production process, a one-customer-one-sale situation. Each sale is a unit by itself, typically taking place away from the office and therefore removed from the point of supervision. It would seem evident that the technology associated with selling life insurance would make autonomy of sales agents an important condition of success.

Evidence is by no means conclusive in support of the contention that worker autonomy is essential for high individual productivity. Indeed, when worker autonomy (of which general supervision instead of close supervision is the foreman facet) is combined with two other dimensions of supervisory behavior found significant in combination in the English factories, the combination still accounts for less than one-fifth of the variance in productivity. Further, there is reason to believe that worker autonomy may be relevant to batch- or unit-production technologies, but probably not to mass-production technologies and almost certainly not to continuous-process technologies.

CONSIDERATION FOR WORKERS AS A GOAL

Another popular goal of supervision is to develop considerate treatment of subordinates. This supervisory stance may be

---

[40] Rensis Likert, *op. cit.* in note 36.

characterized as being employee-centered. The presumption underlying a belief in employee-centered supervision is that considerate treatment will be repaid by devoted effort and possibly higher output.

Kahn reviewed the study of two groups of employees in a large business office, the Prudential study.[41] One group was given employee-centered supervision and the other was given just the opposite. Both groups showed a significant increase in productivity. The employee-centered supervision produced an increase in favorable employee attitudes toward supervisors and the company, while the authoritarian-led group showed a marked decrease in employee satisfaction. This classic study, often cited in support of the employee-centered supervision ethic, provides data to show that employee-centeredness is *not* the critical factor that determines individual productivity. If anything, the most direct conclusion from this study is that productivity can either be forced or be encouraged with about the same outcomes with respect to output. Obviously it is other outcomes that distinguish the two methods of supervision.

Kahn further reported on the heavy-industry study among 20,000 workers engaged in the manufacture of tractors and earth-moving equipment:

Like the earlier studies, the research in the tractor factory showed that the foremen with the best production records were the ones who were most skilled at and most concerned with meeting employee needs for information, support, assistance, but they were no less concerned with production. . . . The foremen with the best production records, in short, were both production-centered and employee-centered.

It is especially desirable to pay attention to one of Kahn's major conclusions:

It thus appeared that the continuum of supervisory behavior which placed employee-centeredness at one end and production-centered-

---

[41] Robert L. Kahn, *op. cit.* in note 34.

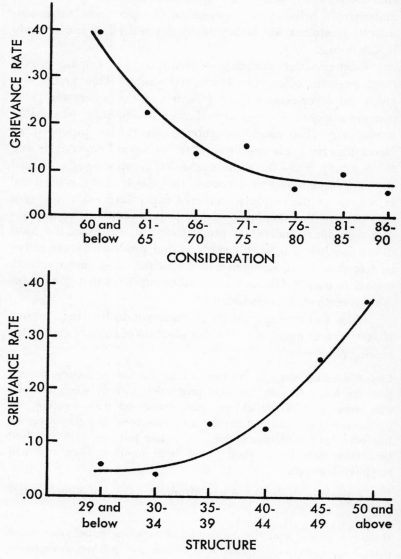

Figure 5 (portion). See legend, facing page.

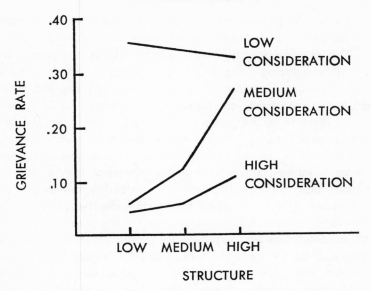

Figure 5. Leadership Behavior and Grievances. (Redrawn from E. A. Fleishman and E. F. Harris, "Patterns of Leadership Behavior Related to Employee Grievances and Turnover," cited in footnote 43.)

ness at the other was less in accord with the facts than a four-fold classification of supervisors which would include two additional types —the supervisor who combined employee and production orientation and the supervisor who gave neither of these emphases to his role.[42]

In the Fleishman, Harris study[43] of 57 foremen in a motor-truck manufacturing plant, it was found that as the degree of consideration shown toward subordinates increased the grievance rate decreased (Figure 5). This decrease is not a straight-line relationship but is a curvilinear one. The greatest amount of

[42] *Ibid.*, pp. 44 and 45.
[43] E. A. Fleishman and E. F. Harris, "Patterns of Leadership Behavior Related to Employee Grievances and Turnover," *Personnel Psychology*, 15:45-53 (1962).

decrease in the grievance rate comes as consideration increases from the lowest levels to near the mid point of consideration.

The structuring of the work relationship as measured on a scale of structuring behaviors by the foremen shows a curve in the opposite direction. The more structure imposed upon work by the supervisor the higher the grievance rate. The most marked increase in the grievance rate occurs only after the mid point in the structuring behavior of the foreman is reached.

However, when the two factors of consideration and structure are combined and related to the grievance rate, a very interesting fact emerges. When low consideration for employees is consistent, then the more structuring the behavior of the foreman the *lower* is the grievance rate. On the other hand, when high consideration for employees is shown consistently by the foreman, then the more the structuring the higher is the grievance rate. The grievance rate goes up most markedly if medium consideration is shown toward employees and structuring goes from low to high.

Employee-turnover rates have a pattern almost exactly like those of grievances when related to foreman consideration and structuring of the work situation. It is again notable that the curvilinear relationships show that the major rate of change in employee turnover occurs at the low end of the consideration scale, with a moderate degree of consideration materially reducing the turnover rate, and with further increase in consideration having no further influence in reducing turnover. Similarly, an increase in structure up to about the mid point produces no increase in turnover, but beyond the mid point it makes for a marked increase in turnover.

This study provides good evidence of the consequences of supervisory behavior for turnover and grievances; but again, it should be emphasized, neither of these have been demonstrated to be directly related to productivity. Multiple goals of supervision are illustrated here and it is demonstrated quite adequately that differences in supervisory practices will produce

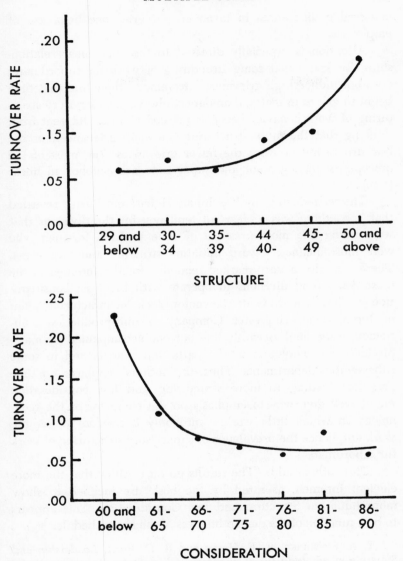

Figure 6. Leadership Behavior and Turnover Rates. (Redrawn from E. A. Fleishman and E. F. Harris, "Patterns of Leadership Behavior Related to Employee Grievances and Turnover," cited in footnote 43.)

measurable differences in turnover and grievance behaviors of employees.

Attention is especially directed to the curvilinear relationships. To know that some structuring of work for subordinates does not induce high grievance rates among them and that they begin to grieve in material amounts only when supervisory structuring of work behavior becomes marked is quite different from thinking that the more structuring the more grievances, or the less structuring of work the fewer grievances. Yet, most of the precepts of management and supervision are couched in linear terms.

The related study by Fleishman, Harris, and Burtt[44] revealed that ". . . there was a clear-cut tendency for the divisions that were under the most pressure of time to have foremen who were most inclined toward initiating structure and vice versa. There was also a very marked tendency for the foremen in the most demanding divisions to operate with the least consideration."[45] This is a study of the motor-truck manufacturing plant of International Harvester Company, a unit-production technology in the final assembly line but one accompanied by mass-production technologies in the parts departments and in some subassembly departments. Thus, the authors' emphasis on time pressures leading to more structuring and less consideration might well give way to emphasis on the character of the technology in which little worker autonomy is needed to get the work out, hence the prevalence of supervisory structuring of work for subordinates.

The authors add: "The results go on to show that the more efficient foremen, as rated by the boss, are inclined to show more initiation Structure and less Consideration. This appears to be a function of the demandingness of the time schedule."[46]

---

[44] E. A. Fleishman, E. F. Harris and R. D. Burtt, *Leadership and Supervision in Industry* (Columbus: Ohio State University Press, 1955).
[45] *Ibid.*, p. 99.   [46] *Ibid.*, p. 99.

The theme that technology affects supervisory behaviors appeared in this early study by Fleishman, Harris, and Burtt. However, neither they nor subsequent analysts recognized what Woodward later discovered. The following quotation explains:

Results indicate that there appears to be a difference between production and non-production departments in the requisite kinds of leadership. [This is one way of stating the difference in this sample between mass-production and unit- or batch-production technologies in Woodward's terms.] In the non-production departments, the foremen who are rated most proficient by their own supervisors apparently motivate their work groups to get the job done by creating a friendly atmosphere and by considerate behavior with a minimum of emphasis on work methods, standards, and structuring of activities. [In production departments foremen play a difficult role. Their] considerate behavior is very good from the morale standpoint, but not so good for proficiency as judged by the foreman's own boss.[47]

In the Fleishman and Peters study[48] of the effectiveness of middle managers in a continuous-production operation, soap and detergent manufacture, 39 managers in the ranks between line foremen and plant managers were studied. The major conclusions are: (1) "there is an absence of relationship between leadership attitudes and rated effectiveness," and (2) "no particular combination of Structure and Consideration attitudes was predictive of effectiveness ratings."[49] Here the managers' efficiency was rated by their own superiors.

Thus, for production workers in unit and small-batch technologies, the factors of high consideration and low structure do have a bearing on rated departmental efficiency and foreman proficiency, if not on output. In mass production, efficiency and effectiveness are positively related to low consideration by the

[47] *Ibid.*, p. 103-104.
[48] E. A. Fleishman and D. R. Peters, "Interpersonal Values, Leadership Attitudes and Managerial 'Success'," *Personnel Psychology*, 15: 127-143 (1962).
[49] *Ibid.*, p. 136.

foreman and much structuring of the work situation by him. In managing middle managers, neither consideration nor structuring relates to rated efficiency of performance.

SENSITIVITY TO WORKERS AS A GOAL

A firmly established notion stemming from the group dynamics tradition has been that supervisors who are sensitive to the needs of their subordinates have an important requisite for being effective leaders. The insensitive supervisor is presumably an ineffective leader. The idea that "sensitivity" is an essential ingredient of supervisory practice has even been incorporated into a formal training program called "sensitivity training."[50]

In a study by Nagle[51] a questionnaire was administered to supervisors to measure their sensitivity, and six plant executives rated departments as to their productivity. Then these data on 14 departments composed of office workers in a large industrial organization were correlated. It was found that there was a correlation of .82 between supervisor sensitivity and rated productivity of the department.

The meaning of "sensitivity" is variously interpreted. According to Fiedler,[52] sensitivity means the ability to discriminate clearly among subordinates on the basis of their characteristics. Thus Cleven and Fiedler,[53] in their study of steel-mill open hearth supervisors, took note of discrimination as exercised by pit foremen and melters, the supervisors most directly involved

---

[50] See the description of "sensitivity training" in Robert Tannenbaum, Fred Massarik, and Irving Weschler, *Leadership and Organization* (New York: McGraw-Hill Book Co., 1961).

[51] B. F. Nagle, "Productivity, Employee Attitude, and Supervisor Sensitivity," *Personnel Psychology*, 7:219-233 (1954).

[52] Fred E. Fiedler, *Leadership Attitudes and Group Effectiveness* (Urbana: University of Illinois Press, 1958) summarizes the several studies made by Fiedler in this area.

[53] W. A. Cleven and Fred E. Fiedler, "Interpersonal Perceptions of Open Hearth Foremen and Steel Production," *Journal of Applied Psychology*, 40:312-314 (1956).

in open-hearth operations. They found that those whose crews had good production records discriminated more sharply between the most- and the least-liked coworkers; those whose crew production records were below average discriminated less sharply.

This meaning of sensitivity, sensitivity to the differences among subordinates and the ability to use this information effectively to supervise them, may be the factor which accounts for the high correlation that Nagle found between supervisor's sensitivity and the attributed productivity of his group. The Cleven and Fiedler results were obtained in a batch-production situation and the Nagle results in a unit-production technology (office work). These are similar technologies and demand high worker autonomy. The results of the two studies may legitimately be put together to support the opinion that in such a technology sensitivity to the individual characteristics of the worker is one of the supervisor traits which is successful in getting a high level of productivity from workers. That is, the supervisor may well give different kinds of autonomy to individual workers in accord with their special personalities and other characteristics. The more successful supervisor may be the one best able to perceive these individual characteristics (discriminate them, in Fiedler's terms) in order to tailor his own actions to the individual's unique qualities.

WORKER PARTICIPATION AS A GOAL

A particularly important study in the analysis of supervisory practices was that by French and Coch,[54] in which the effects of employee participation in a decision affecting them were measured. It was concluded that those who participated in decisions regarding work changes ultimately reached somewhat higher levels of output than a comparable group of workers who were told to change their methods of work. This study has

---

[54] Lester Coch and John R. P. French, Jr., "Overcoming Resistance to Change," *Human Relations*, 1:512-532 (1948).

been the cornerstone of theory concluding that worker participation is desirable for efficiency reasons and improvement of output levels.

Wickert[55] studied employee turnover and feelings of ego involvement in the day-to-day operations of telephone operators and female service representatives in the Michigan Bell Telephone Company. About 700 women were studied. The principal finding was that those who stayed with the company had a greater feeling of involvement in the day-to-day operations of the company than those who left. Specifically, those who stayed tended to say (1) they had a chance to make decisions on the job, and (2) they felt they were making an important individual contribution to the success of the company. It will be noted that telephone operators and service representatives are all involved in unit production, since they each have to depend upon someone initiating a call or a service request before they go into action. Under these circumstances of technology a material degree of autonomy is probably essential in maintaining levels of output. A chance to make decisions on the job and contribute to company success are measures of participation. It might be concluded, however, that these aspects of participation in work are mediated by the need for autonomy that comes from the technology employed.

In Rice's study of the Indian weaving shed,[56] a comparison was made of production before and after a change in the organization of the work. The individual workers in the experimental weaving groups revised the production process from what had previously been a confused and relatively unstructured one. The data demonstrate that the subsequent steady state of output was markedly and significantly higher after the workers reorganized the work themselves. Furthermore, the rate of cloth

[55] F. R. Wickert, "Turnover and Employee's Feelings of Ego-Involvement," *Personnel Psychology*, 4:185-197 (1951).

[56] A. K. Rice, "Productivity and Social Organization in an Indian Weaving Shed," *Human Relations*, 6:297-329 (1953).

damage in the weaving mill was lower than before reorganization of production.

Several comments need to be made about this study. The self-organizing productive groups increased their efficiency by about 18 per cent if we take the before-reorganization figures as the base. This improvement tends to give the impression, as Rice suggests, that the self-organization of work is one means for increasing efficiency considerably. But a disturbing feature of this situation also must be taken into account. The original structuring of the work situation, which continued to obtain in the nonexperimental groups in the same company, was one in which there were confused task and worker relationships, and no perceptible internal work-group structure. Thus the base from which change was measured in this study may be an instance of industrial "anarchy," or near anarchy, in which the designs of the production processes themselves were scarcely adequate.

Under these circumstances, any attention to the *organization* of work, whether management-initiated or worker-initiated, undoubtedly would have produced significant increases in productivity. Weaving, being a continuous-process production technology over short time spans, would require high structure for adequate performance. In the light of Fleishman's results it seems probable that structuring itself is what may have improved productivity in the Indian weaving shed, not worker participation. It may not, therefore, be desirable or warranted to draw the conclusion that high autonomy and participation in decisions by the Indian weavers are what really produced higher output.

Likert, in an early paper,[57] made the point that

Available research findings indicate, therefore, that when . . . the amount of participation used is less than or very much greater than

---

[57] Rensis Likert, "Effective Supervision: An Adaptive and Relative Process," *op. cit.*, p. 329.

expected, an unfavorable reaction is likely to be evoked. Substantially greater amounts of participation than expected appear to exceed the skill of the subordinate to cope with it and produce a negative reaction because of the threatening nature of the situation to the subordinate. The available theory and research findings suggest that the best results obtain when the amount of participation used is somewhat greater than expected by the subordinate, but still within their capacity to respond to it effectively.

Likert had made this point as early as 1952, but it is a point that is rarely given attention by those who urge participative management as the be-all and end-all of supervisory practice.

Likert clearly argued for an optimal rather than a maximal level of participation of subordinates in decision making relative to their own destinies. That is, there is a curvilinear relation between worker participation and such consequences as output. This relation recalls Fleishman's studies of initiating structure and consideration which relate in a curvilinear fashion to turnover and absenteeism. That is to say, over part of the range of consideration and initiating structure for subordinates there is no material change in their reactions, but beyond a critical point their reactions become prompt and decisive.

The general conclusion that emerges is that employee participation is probably not linearly related but rather curvilinearly related to aspects of working behavior. Likert has pointed out that his own researches have indicated that supervisory behavior in excess of normal expectations will not be favorably accepted by subordinates. This disfavor may be particularly likely if the supervisor invites participation beyond the subordinate's normal level of acceptance. This conclusion recalls Barnard's "zone of indifference," in which reactions of the subordinate become significant only if the supervisor exceeds the tolerance limits customarily adopted by the subordinate.[58]

---

[58] Chester I. Barnard, *The Functions of the Executive* (Cambridge, Mass.: Harvard University Press, 1938).

REWARDING WORKERS AS A GOAL

One of the important functions of supervisors is that of rewarding subordinates. In modern industrial firms the immediate supervisor has relatively little connection with monetary rewards, except perhaps to recommend promotions and pay increases. There remains, however, a range of nonfinancial rewards that each supervisor can monitor in influencing his subordinates. Surprisingly little research has been directed at finding out what effects such rewards have.

In the interesting study by Zaleznik, Christensen, and Roethlisberger,[59] 50 industrial workers were analyzed to determine the influences of social factors on productivity. Among the major findings was the fact that individuals with high status and high status congruence (agreement between self-conception and other's perception that they are properly placed in a social system) tended to produce at the normal or expected levels of output more than they tended to deviate from "on-line" output. On the other hand, of individuals with low status and low status congruence twice as many were deviant in output as were "on-line."

In analyzing status by itself it was found that the high-status people were average in productivity and "on-line" more than they deviated, while the low-status people deviated more than they were "on-line" in output. However, when status congruence was examined by itself the relationship turned out to be nonsignificant between that and level of productivity.

The study showed that when both management and the peer group rewarded the workers, more of them produced "on-line" than were deviant by a ratio of 8 to 3. Similarly when management did not reward the worker but the group did, more produced "on-line" by the ratio of 6 to 3. However, when manage-

[59] Abe Zaleznik, Charles R. Christensen, and Fritz J. Roethlisberger, *The Motivation, Productivity, and Satisfaction of Workers* (Cambridge, Mass.: Harvard University Press, 1958).

ment rewarded the individual and the group did not, or when neither rewarded, then the preponderance was deviancy by the individual from the "on-line" expectations of output. When management alone rewarded the worker, he tended to produce below norm. When neither rewarded the worker, however, he tended to produce above average.

Another way of examining the influences of the social factors on productivity is to look at the character of group membership and its impact on productivity. Those who were regular members of a group tended to produce in the ratio of 14 at the expected average to 6 "off-line." Those who were perceived by the group as being deviant individuals were predominantly "off-line" in output in the ratio of 10 to 3 who were "on-line," while isolates from the group tended to produce "off-line" in the ratio of 9 to 3 who were "on-line." Thus, being a deviant or isolate from the work group meant that the individual would not produce at the expected norm of output. It is interesting to note that those who were deviants from the work group tended to produce higher than the norm, while those who were isolates from the work group tended to produce below standard.

These results, suggestive as they are, must be approached cautiously since the numbers on which they are based are small, there being only 45 workers in the total sample for whom full data were available. The conclusions can be treated as suggesting the following speculations.

It seems that individual productivity is influenced by (1) the location of an individual in a social group, (2) the status accorded to him by those in his social environment, and (3) the sources of social rewards coming to him. The smallness of the sample precludes any cross tabulations to isolate the impact of rewards vs. social position when these factors are considered simultaneously.

What seems especially notable is that individual productivity varies with social factors in the work situation that may not be within the influence range of the supervisor. Indeed, strange as it may seem, insofar as supervisors manipulate non-financial rewards without parallel rewards coming from the peer work group, the worker response may be output lower than the norm! This finding is significant for reinforcement theorists in the realm of industrial incentives. Complicating the reinforcement theorist's problem even further is the finding that nonreward produces output higher than normal! Maybe if we really want high productivity, the social payoffs with which we reward industrial workers should be withheld!

The study just analyzed calls attention to the importance of the working peer group as a source of reward and reinforcement of individual behavior. This importance turns attention to the characteristics of peer groups. Among those features studied that bear on productivity is peer-group cohesiveness.

Seashore's study[60] of group cohesiveness in the industrial work group showed (Figure 7) that among low-productivity groups, worker-perceived pressure for productivity decreased as the group cohesiveness increased. When the condition of maximum group cohesiveness was approached the perceived degree of pressure for productivity went up markedly. This tendency contrasted with that in groups of high productivity, which perceived a declining degree of pressure for productivity as group cohesiveness increased.

For the low-productivity group, management pressure for productivity was perceived only if the group was highly cohesive. Thus, one of the consequences of cohesiveness in low-productivity groups is to provide the opportunity for supportive rebellion against management. This conclusion is further supported by the general summing up by Seashore: "High cohesive groups differ more frequently and in greater amount than low cohesive groups from the plant norms of productivity. These deviations are toward both high and lower productivity."[61]

[60] Stanley E. Seashore, *op. cit.*

[61] *Ibid.,* p. 98.

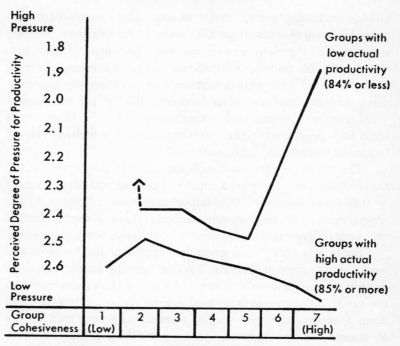

Figure 7. Relationship between Group Cohesiveness and Perceived Degree of Pressure for Productivity. The measure of perceived degree of pressure for productivity is based on response to the question, "How hard do you usually have to work in order to get your work done?" A high numerical score represents relatively low pressure. (Redrawn from Stanley Seashore, *Group Cohesiveness in the Industrial Work Group,* cited in footnote 31.)

CONCLUSION

Supervision does make some difference in productivity. Supervisory practices also affect other aspects of work. The details of these conclusions depart significantly from current views, and are both unique and surprising.

1. Supervisory behavior affects the productivity of individuals by being appropriate to the work setting. One key to describing the characteristics of work settings is to know the nature of the technologies employed. The descriptive task has just

begun but the results are promising. By drawing simple distinctions between unit- and mass-production technologies, and viewing continuous production as another type of technology, supervisory styles are found appropriate to each technological type. The more a production process resembles a unit or batch technology, the greater is the probability that worker autonomy and its supervisory counterpart—general rather than close supervision —will be appropriate. The more a technology resembles a continuous-production system the more appropriate will close supervision be.

2. This first proposition leads directly to the second. There is no "one best" method of supervision. As in all human systems, there is variability in the systems of supervision of industrial and commercial work. Several styles of supervision are effective, but they are individually successful only in relation to appropriate work settings. Variety in supervisory behaviors may no longer be considered a challenge to choose the "one best" for all settings, but rather as a challenge to understand where each does or does not work.

3. As far as empirical data take us, it seems clear that the influence of supervisory behaviors on *productivity* is small. The studies are few in number, however, and not adequately designed to measure magnitude of influence of supervision on productivity.

4. Supervison of industrial and commercial work has many functions. The variety of areas in which supervisors act is the consequence of their having numerous functional contributions to make. For a given situation supervision may have relatively little to do with individual productivity, and yet supervisors, because they perform many other functions, may retain importance in work organizations. Executives must therefore constantly face the difficult problem of organizational design and the choice of operating goals for supervisors. If, for example, top management wants workers to be happy this goal may be attained by appropriate supervisory behaviors.

5. The goals of supervision and the behaviors of supervisors are independent of each other in one sense and linked in another. A variety of goals may be assigned to supervisors, and those selected do not appear to be limited or determined by any features of organizational structure or process. Thus, consideration of workers may be emphasized in unit production, in mass production, or in process production if top management chooses consideration as a goal. Supervisory practices in each technological system will be different although directed toward the same goal. It is in this sense that the goals of supervision and the behaviors of supervisors are independent of each other.

On the other hand, goals and behaviors are linked through technology since behaviors necessary to achieve a particular goal must be appropriate to the operating situation. For example, consideration of workers in unit-production technologies may exhibit itself by providing workers with maximum opportunities to pace their own work, while in continuous-production technologies the same consideration may be most appropriately expressed as detailed concern with safety or physical comfort of the worker.

6. It is now possible to take a sophisticated view of the impact of supervision on working behaviors. Most analysts up to this time have assumed that whatever the linkage, it tended to be a linear one. That is, a unit change in a particular supervisory behavior was assumed to produce a corresponding change in worker response throughout the range of supervisory action. This view is simply false. Many behaviors have thresholds above which the behavior is responded to by others, but below which the behaviors produce little or no effect. Thresholds were revealed, for example, in the relationship between supervisory consideration and worker responses in terms of grievances and absenteeism. This phenomenon was also discovered in the relation between opportunity to participate in decisions and worker responses to the opportunity.

7. A supervisory practice in the low range may have one

effect on worker response, but in the high range may produce exactly the opposite effect. This disparity was exhibited in the consequence of supervisory pressure for worker morale. At least in some demonstrable instances the relationship between supervisory behavior and worker response is nonlinear and may even be parabolic. Evidence supports the contention that if a little bit of a supervisory behavior may be good, a lot may be very bad indeed. This optimization notion is sometimes overlooked in the theory and practice of personnel administration.

8. An important technological trend is making for a fundamental shift in industry from the management of people to the management of things. The detailed study of continuous-process manufacture showed the highest ratio of managers to other workers for any type of technology. It has been inferred that this high ratio reflects the need for supervisor surveillance of high-speed production processes to insure that product runs are error-free, since large numbers of defects can be produced by the time the process is halted to correct an error. As supervisors supervise machines more and people less, they will become increasingly responsible for production. Supervisory controls will not be controls on speed of output, since output will be machine- or process-paced. The supervisors will be largely concerned with controlling quality, and the operating contingencies that influence the go-no-go performance of the production process.

9. Knowledge of leadership and supervision as they affect working behavior is almost exclusively the result of studying American industrial practices. A few important English studies have been cited here, and additional studies dealing with other national economies are scattered through the literature.[62] Cul-

---

[62] I cite just two studies conducted in Scandinavian countries which have been scarcely noticed by American scholars although both are significant contributions. K. Raino, *Leadership Qualities: A Theoretical Inquiry and an Experimental Study of Foremen* (Helsinki: Annales Academiae Scientiarum Fennicae, Series B, vol. 95.1, 1955); Uno Remitz, *Professional Satisfaction among Swedish Bank Employees* (Copenhagen: Munksgaard, 1960).

ture does make a difference in supervisory practices. It follows, then, that caution is necessary in applying present knowledge to cultural settings different from those in which the knowledge was gained. Generalizations may work universally, but then again they may not. We have no *a priori* reason for guessing which of these two outcomes will obtain.

10. All the studies of human relations and supervision tell little about how much productivity is affected by individual supervisory practices. Only one study attempted to tease out the answer to this question and it suggested that not more than one-fifth of the variance in productivity can be accounted for by a combination of three supervisory practices. The Western Electric and other researches showed that fellow workers influence the individual's output. Advances in technology produce steady increases in man-hour productivity. There has never been a proper analysis of variance to assay that relative importance of simultaneous factors affecting individual output. It is certainly time to turn empirical attention to just this kind of problem.

2

Effort, Supervision, and

Productivity

GEORGE C. HOMANS

Two questions are involved: (1) How much of the variance in human productivity can be attributed to human effort? (2) How much of this variance can be further accounted for by the specific form of effort called supervision?

These questions at once require rephrasing. First, *productivity* is often measured as a rate, such as the number of units of a product manufactured per some unit of cost. Indeed there are any number of different ways of measuring productivity, appropriate in different circumstances. I shall use the number of units produced within some—usually unstated—period of time. This measure is better called *production* than *productivity*. Second, what is meant by human *effort?* It is possible to measure the amount of metabolic energy a man puts into work but only under special laboratory conditions. For all practical purposes, the only measure we have of a man's effort is the actual amount of work he, together with his tool or machine, produces in a given period of time. That is, his effort is measured by his production. It looks as if there were not two variables but only one. I shall call this variable human *activity* rather than human *effort,* and define it as the frequency within a given period of time with

51

which a man carries out a sequence of activities that accomplish
some specified end result. Activity is very difficult to measure
for any complex kind of intellectual work, and so I shall confine myself to simple, repetitive, clerical and manual operations
that accomplish such end-results as the assembly of some piece
of equipment or the accounting for the payment of a block of
bills.

EFFORT IN GENERAL

The first question then becomes: How much of the variance
in human production can be attributed to human activity? The
answer is in one sense easy and in another very difficult. The
easy answer is that every single bit of variance in human production is due to human activity. To this assertion a critic would
reply that, throughout history, by far the largest changes in, for
instance, industrial production have been due, not to any increase
in the effort made by industrial workers themselves, but to the
introduction of new methods of production and new machinery
and to increases in the amount of mechanical, animal, thermal,
electrical, and atomic power used in the industrial process. This
statement is true, and it is the first and most obvious fact we
must bear in mind. Indeed the amount of activity per man
put into the industrial process has tended to decrease, at least
in the sense of the number of hours worked, though even that
must be qualified. Thus the number of hours a day an English
weaver worked during the Middle Ages was strictly limited by
the hours of daylight, which were few indeed during the winter.

On the other hand, the introduction of new machinery and
more power are themselves the result of human activity. What
is more, they do not eliminate human activity. To be as obvious as possible: a new machine does not increase production un·
less someone is ready to tend it. This truism is just as true under
automation as it ever was. That is, the increases in production
brought about by new capital investments depend on the condition that some minimum degree of human effort is forthcoming.

Indeed, the actual increases in production resulting from these factors are, in the beginning at least, seldom as great as they theoretically ought to be. But if machinery and power cannot eliminate human activity, they do of course reduce the proportion of total production attributable to immediate activity, as distinguished from the activity that went into the production of the capital goods. When a man worked with his hands alone, all the variance in his production could be attributed to his immediate efforts and to environmental conditions. Every industrial advance has reduced the proportion.

The more difficult answer is really an answer to a different question: Given that machinery, methods, and power remain constant, what variations in production are due to human activity? Or rather, since under the given conditions the variations in production must be due to human activity, what in fact are these variations?

The answers to this question must be empirical and circumstantial and not theoretical and general. We cannot easily compare variations in production at different kinds of work, for in some kinds the degree to which workers can increase their production is limited. It is limited when the work is machine-paced, as on an assembly line, though of course the observation that men have time on their hands may lead to the speeding up of the line. We cannot easily compare production at the same kind of work in different factories, for we can have little confidence that the other determinants of production are the same. We cannot easily compare individual variations in production at the same kind of work in the same factory, for these may be due—though they certainly are not always due—to individual variations in skill and experience. What we can reasonably do is take particular departments of particular plants and ask what increases in the average production of the workers have been observed—methods, machinery, and power remaining constant. But even here the results depend on the base line of production from which the increase was measured. A group that is already working hard will have a hard time increasing production even more.

I shall confine myself to some of the evidence from American industry. There is, by the way, very little evidence that, other things equal, sheer cultural differences between peoples play a part in their rate of working. In American industry it has sometimes been estimated for working groups where restriction of output prevails that, if men skilled at the job worked at a rate limited only by what they could physically sustain, they could often double production—an increase of 100 per cent.[1] But this estimate is based on a condition contrary to fact. The actually observed increases have been much smaller. In an unpublished study made by the methods of participant observation a student of mine found that welders could produce at a rate about 30 per cent higher than the standard set by time study.[2] Coch and French in their experiment in a pajama factory obtained increases in production, compared with their control group, of about 40 per cent.[3] Perhaps the best evidence is provided by the celebrated Relay Assembly Test Room in the Western Electric researches. I suspect that the girls in this group were already working pretty hard while they were in their original department. But at least there is every reason to believe that in the Test Room they became strongly motivated to do their best. Under these circumstances, the individual girls in the course of two years increased their average hourly outputs by amounts ranging between 20 and 60 per cent.[4]

In short, we cannot say how much of the variance in human productivity is attributable to human effort. In a sense it

[1] George C. Homans, *Fatigue of Workers* (New York: Reinhold Publishing Co., 1941), p. 118.

[2] S. Robbins, *Human Factors in Industrial Output* (unpublished undergraduate honors thesis, Harvard University, 1948).

[3] Lester Coch and John R. P. French, Jr., "Overcoming Resistance to Change," *Human Relations*, 1:512-532 (1948).

[4] Fritz J. Roethlisberger and W. J. Dickson, *Management and the Worker* (Cambridge: Harvard University Press, 1939), p. 76.

all is. What we can do is to observe the changes in productivity that might have occurred, or actually did occur, among fully skilled workers while carrying out their old tasks without any change in methods, machinery, or power. For American industry the evidence is that most of the increases lie between 20 per cent and 100 per cent of the production before the increase. To put the matter in another way: the general level of effort is such that workers, by making greater efforts, could not in most cases more than double their production. I am not saying that such an increase, if actually made and maintained, would be an absolutely small one. If it were general throughout a firm (and all the actual evidence is concerned with single departments), it might well make the difference between bankruptcy and a satisfactory profit. If it were general throughout the economy it would create enormous problems of unemployment. What I am saying is that an increase of this order is relatively small in comparison with the long-term increases brought about by investment in new methods, machinery, and sources of power.

SUPERVISORY EFFORT

Having given this very unsatisfactory answer to the first question, I now turn to the second: How much of the variance in productivity due to human effort can be further accounted for by the specific form of effort called supervision? Just as we cannot say that productivity can be broken down into one part that is due to human effort and another that is due to methods, machinery, and power, since if no human effort were expended the machines would be useless, so we cannot in general say that a particular amount of variation in productivity is due to supervision alone, since there are circumstances in which bad supervision can account for all the variance in productivity. Thus the master of a fine ship with a good crew can, by giving a wrong order, cause the total loss of ship and crew. Here the supervisor's behavior resulted in negative productivity for the unit. And the same sort of thing can be true of the foreman of a rolling mill or a blast furnace or a coal face. Of course you may choose to consider the supervisor's behavior in these cases to be technical and not truly supervisory. But note that the error is made in giving orders to others, and what is that but supervision?

On the other side, consider again the Relay Assembly Test Room. What part of the increase in productivity could be attributed to supervision? In a sense it all could, since supervision in the largest view created the conditions in which the workers then proceeded to increase output. It was the combination of supervision and worker behavior that produced increased output, and it is meaningless to ask what proportion each contributed.

This example raises the question what is meant by supervision. If it encompasses all members of management including the president and the board of directors, then it is clear that supervision makes a great deal of difference to productivity. Among other things it is top management that decides whether or not to make new capital investments. Not only that—it decides, in negotiation with the union, what the wage and promotion policies shall be, and these have a vital bearing on the production of individual workers. Finally, it helps determine by its official policies and even more by its actual behavior—by the way it treats its first-line supervisors—how they in turn behave in immediate contact with the work force. If I had to choose I should say that top management made more difference to production than any other single factor.

But I suspect that the higher levels of management are not what we usually mean when we speak of supervision. Let us narrow the question down, as we narrowed the first question, and consider only first-line supervision in routine American clerical and manufacturing operations. Let us again assume methods, machinery, and power constant. Under these conditions let us ask how great are the observed variations in productivity that are associated with variations in the behavior of first-line supervisors.

It is difficult to get information on this point. Mind you, there are several studies, particularly those made by the Survey Research Center of the University of Michigan, showing that high-producing work groups are statistically more likely than low-producing ones to have supervisors whose behavior seems "good" to the investigators, notably in being democratic, nonpunitive, employee-centered, and "general" (not breathing down the workers' necks).[5] In these findings, there is always some question which variable was the independent one. Thus a supervisor taking over a group that is already high in production may have the less reason to breathe down their necks. Did the supervisor's behavior change the productivity, or vice versa? But this is not the present question. We want to know, not whether one group under one kind of supervision produces more than another group under another kind of supervision, but *how much more* it produces. The research findings could hold good, and yet the actual amount of differences in productivity be small.

It is surprising how little evidence there is on this point. In fact there is only one piece of research I know of that tries to answer the question in any general way. Michael Argyle and his colleagues, after surveying the literature and making their own independent studies, concluded that "good" supervision in the Michigan sense was indeed associated with increased productivity, but cautioned "that the differences in productivity in work groups resulting from contrasting methods of supervision were typically small, usually not larger than 15 per cent of the total output."[6]

This finding may come as a shock to many Americans, who hold the endearing belief that actions defined as good ought to

---

[5] For a useful summary, see Rensis Likert, *New Patterns of Management* (New York: McGraw-Hill Book Co., 1961).

[6] Michael Argyle, Godfrey Gardner, and Frank Ciofi, "Supervisory Methods Related to Production, Absenteeism, and Labor Turnover," *Human Relations*, 11:23-40 (1958), cited in Peter M. Blau and W. Richard Scott, *Formal Organizations* (San Francisco: Chandler Publishing Company, 1962), p. 151.

make a big difference. But 15 per cent of total output is not a really big difference, even though such an increase, if general throughout American industry, would save billions of dollars. Why do companies and industrial sociologists worry so much about supervision when the differences resulting from good supervision are so small? We might argue that increasing productivity is not the only job of the supervisor, and that we should press for better supervision, even if it had no effect on productivity at all, so long as it increased the satisfactions of the workers. Yet it is sometimes true that "good" supervision in the Michigan sense, while increasing productivity, decreases satisfaction. Men left free of detailed supervision in doing their jobs may increase their production but come to feel that the high degree of responsibility they have exercised warrants their getting an increase in pay. If they do not get it, they will be more dissatisfied than men who were never given the freedom in the first place.[7] Management creates problems for itself by its wisdom as well as by its folly and is sometimes less well prepared to meet them. Perhaps the best argument for our concern with supervision is that, if we did not try to make it better, the average would not remain even as good as it is.

But perhaps the 15 per cent is misleading. Remember this is a figure based largely on information about first-line supervisors. Perhaps we were wrong in focusing on first-line supervision. The behavior of foremen alone may not make much specific difference, and yet the behavior of total supervision, of the whole management, may make a very great difference indeed. Indeed I argue that this is the case, and that it is even more the case in modern industry than it was in the past.

SOURCES OF AUTHORITY

The reason why present-day supervisors seem to make so little difference in changing the production of the men under

---

[7] Nancy C. Morse, *Satisfactions in the White-Collar Job* (Ann Arbor: Survey Research Center, 1953), p. 138.

their command is that in fact they have little power to do so. This conclusion is seldom stated, though it follows directly from the most obvious findings of behavioral psychology. We expect results from foremen who have not the means of attaining them, and we are continually surprised by their lack of success.

Let us consider the general problem of leadership in small groups. A leader is a man whose orders, whether implicit or explicit, are in fact obeyed by those to whom he directs them. One important order, often left implicit, is the supervisor's order to his men: "Work hard!" But there are obviously degrees of leadership or, as I shall say, of authority. I shall say that a leader has more authority, the larger the number of men who obey his orders, the more fully they do so, and over a wider range of activities. These are different dimensions, and authority may vary independently over each of them; but to keep the exposition simple I shall assume it varies concomitantly.

The next question is what the factors are that determine the degree of the leader's authority.

1. *Alternative rewards.* Since the probability that men will perform an activity varies with the value to them of the rewards they get from performance, and since an order specifies an activity to be performed, a leader's authority is greater the more valuable the rewards he provides for performance, and the more often he provides them. The relative value of the rewards he provides decreases with the value of alternative rewards that his subordinates can secure by activities other than obedience to his orders. The factor of alternative rewards leads to factor 2.

2. *Power.* A leader's authority is greater the more fully he monopolizes the capacity to provide the rewards and punishments that his subordinates can obtain from their activities. The degree of monopolization is the degree to which he alone is the source of rewards open to his subordinates, the degree to which there are no rewards alternative to those he provides. Remember that the monopoly of the power to punish is also a monopoly of the power to reward, since the monopoly of punish-

ment is the monopoly of the power to withold punishment, and this is rewarding. At the same time, the use of punishment or the threat thereof is unlikely to have just the same effect as of reward, since it arouses reactions of escape and emotional hostility. The degree of monopoly of reward and punishment is the power factor in authority.

3. *Success.* Since the probability that a man will perform an activity depends on his past experience in getting rewards upon the performance of that activity, a leader's authority is greater the more often in the past experience of his followers their obedience to his orders has brought them reward. They need not have been rewarded by the leader himself. If obedience to his orders has resulted in their getting rewarded by other persons or the physical environment, they are likely to obey the leader's orders in the future. This factor in authority may have nothing to do with the leader's power as defined above. He himself may have no power to reward or punish his followers, and still have great authority. If, for example, a man has told you where to find fish, and for any reason you have gone there and found good fishing, you are highly likely on the next occasion to follow any suggestion he may make about fishing. He has increased his authority over you, though he may have no power over you. This I shall call the success factor in authority.

4. *Shared values.* A leader's authority is greater the larger the number of his followers that find rewarding the same results that he does; that is, the larger the number whose values are similar to his own. This factor is particularly important when the rewarding results can only be obtained by the combined efforts of the followers. For then, if any one follower disobeys an order of the leader designed to obtain these results, his action is a threat to the others, who may be counted on to present, implicitly or explicitly, the counterthreat of withholding social rewards—approval, interaction—from the disobedient person. This counterthreat is apt to be the more effective the longer the followers have been together. For instance, unless the members of

a group have built up some degree of liking for one another, they have no liking to withhold from the disobedient member.

5. *Justice.* Finally, a leader's authority is apt to be greater the more fully his behavior in distributing rewards and punishments to his followers has realized the condition of distributive justice, as they see it. Distributive justice is the condition in which rewards and punishments are seen as proportional to contributions or failures in making contributions. The reason why this factor is important is that distributive *in*justice, another word for which is relative deprivation, is apt to arouse anger, and the emotional state of anger is one in which any activity that hurts the source of the injustice is apt to be rewarding. In the case of the unjust leader, disobedience to his orders is often seen as just such an activity.

Each of these factors is related to the others. Unless, for instance, the leader has enough initial power over his men, he may not get them to obey his orders sufficiently to accomplish a joint result that they would then find rewarding. That is, he may not command enough power to bring success into play, and so bolster his authority further. But I need not dwell on these obvious interrelationships.

Nor shall I dwell on the feedback effects of authority on a leader. Thus an order not given is an order that cannot be obeyed. But giving an order is an activity that does not differ from other activities in following the laws of psychology. The probability that an activity will be performed depends on the value of the reward and the degree of its success in getting the reward. Thus a leader whose orders are not obeyed is likely to give fewer orders in the future.

LIMITATIONS ON AUTHORITY

Having made this brief sketch of the general sources of authority, I now return to the special case of the first-line supervisor in American industry. If it can be shown that he commands these sources in a low degree, the fact would go far to explain why his behavior makes so little difference, relatively, to productivity. And it can be shown, at least in the sense that he can do less to control these sources than could his predecessor, the foreman in nineteenth-century industry. Let us take up, one by one, the factors in authority.

The foreman no longer hires, pays, promotes, demotes, or fires his men. Payment is determined by wage policies and incentive schemes set by other departments in the company, specialized in this work. True, the foreman can recommend for promotions and demotions, but union rules about seniority and bumping are apt to have a good deal to say about what actually happens. I am not for one moment denying that these powers were taken away from the foreman for good and sufficient reasons. One of the reasons the unions have insisted on seniority rules has been fear of favoritism (distributive injustice) on the part of foremen. But alas! you cannot have things both ways: you cannot give a man power without also giving him the opportunity to abuse his power. Or to put the matter the other way, you cannot limit his capacity for abusing his power without limiting the power itself. Nor am I saying that the rewards and punishments that affect the behavior of workers have been eliminated. They certainly have not. What I am saying is that the control of these rewards has been distributed through the company (and the union), and that a relatively smaller part of the control still lies in the hands of the foreman himself. Such monopoly of power over his men as he once had has been broken.

Some of the most important kinds of rewards and punishments that might affect production are no longer the foreman's to bestow. I do not mean that he is left without any, or that what he has left is unimportant. But look at what they are: he can praise, he can take a personal interest in his men, he can provide the very important reward of giving them autonomy, not breathing down their necks, and he can to some extent protect them against abrupt and arbitrary changes made by higher management. It is no accident that these things—the democratic or employee-centered form of supervision—are precisely the things that the foremen of high-producing groups are seen as providing. In effect, these foremen successfully use, to get production, the only rewards they still command. And it is interesting that they are seen as having *more* power than the heads of low-producing groups, even if they are not seen by the workers as having *much* power.[8] It is always surprising to be reminded what high morale old-fashioned supervisors, who used few of the methods we now consider appropriate, were often able to create. The surprise results from forgetting that they had more rewards and punishments to create morale with. It is also true that, with the changing culture of America, the character of the work force has changed. Few workingmen today would be ready to take, without humiliation, some of the methods of supervision that were quite appropriate before World War I.

Another characteristic of the old-fashioned foreman made it likely that his subordinates would find obedience to his orders rewarding and so tended to make that obedience habitual. He had often been promoted from the ranks in an industry whose technology was more traditional than it is today. He was apt to have worked up through all the jobs in his department and to be wholly familiar with each one. He could show a newcomer how to do all the jobs and give him directions that he was apt to find useful. His subordinates became habituated to taking orders from him as the best man of the gang.

The modern supervisor is much more apt to have come into his job from the outside. In any event, he is apt to be faced with a rapidly changing technology; many of his subordinates will know their jobs just as well as he does—indeed both are often dependent on staff instructions. Again, all of these things have happened for good and sufficient reasons, but not even the best of inventions is ever introduced without cost—though I some-

---

[8] Rensis Likert, *New Patterns of Management, op. cit.* in note 5, p. 56.

times think Americans believe that if something is really good it should not cost anything. The cost in this case is that the foreman can no longer, by using his experience to help the men in the immediate day-by-day technical problems of their work, build up an habitual willingness to submit to his judgment.

The value of the reward to be obtained from any activity depends on the value of the reward to be obtained by alternative activities, forgone in performing the chosen one. It is the difference between the two values that counts. Even if the foreman in modern industry could himself provide high rewards for working hard, which he cannot, the alternative rewards of not working hard increase rapidly with any increase in production. Even if we admit that, under piece work, the workers' fear that the rate will actually be cut is largely unjustified, still their more general fear that "something would happen" is quite rational. What would happen if in an ordinary department in American industry the workers did actually double production? Nothing could be more devastating. The assembly line that the department fed would be unbalanced by a deluge of parts. The time-study men would swarm in trying to find out what was wrong. The men who could not work so rapidly would be "shown up." Some members of the working group would be transferred if not demoted. I am not saying this in criticism of higher management. I am only pointing out the obvious—that to get high production one must be prepared to reward it, probably to increase the reward progressively with every increment of production, and higher management may not be ready or able to provide the rewards. Given the complicated intermeshing of processes which is modern industry, the company may be able to pay off any one department's high production in a big way, in money or promotions, only if the company as a whole is expanding rapidly; and I hardly need to point out that rapid expansion is far from easy to achieve. Once again, the possibilities of reward in any one area depend increasingly on the behavior of the organization as a whole. I am not saying that organization is more centralized than it used to be, but that the interlocking of its different aspects, including its incentive system, is more complicated.

This complexity further means that one of the factors that may support the authority of a leader, the pressure that other followers bring to bear on a disobedient individual because they share the leader's values, is unlikely to be available to foremen in American industry, at least when they ask for big increases in production. As we know, the really high producers in American industry are apt to be isolates in their groups, real individualists, opposed to management as well as to the group.[9]

Finally, the conditions of justice are largely beyond the control of the supervisor himself. For distributive justice is a matter of the distribution of rewards and punishments, and so far as the rewards themselves are beyond the control of the supervisor, their just distribution is beyond his control too. If some individual or group sees itself at an unfair disadvantage as compared with another, the reason usually lies in some feature of the job evaluation or promotion system that lies beyond the direct control of the supervisor. If it is to be corrected, higher authority and the union must act. To be sure, the supervisor can make representations to higher authority. Indeed the workers expect him to do so—a rather pathetic expectation in view of the fact that his representations may put him in the position of questioning the orders of higher authority. The result is that, in the matter of justice, the foreman is still limited to small change, distributing praise and blame, distributing grants of small requests, such as time off for one reason or another. Even so, the importance of the administration of distributive justice cannot be overestimated. In my experience, the highest praise that a worker can give the foreman is to say, "He's fair."[10] But if the foreman

---

[9] Melville Dalton, "The Industrial Rate-Buster: A Characterization," *Applied Anthropology,* 7:5-18 (1948).

[10] See T. T. Paterson, *Glasgow Limited* (Cambridge: Cambridge University Press, 1960), Chapter 21.

can do little to maintain just conditions, he bears the brunt of injustices established and maintained by the larger organization. For perceived injustice makes rewarding any activity that hurts the source of the injustice; and to withdraw what the source wants is as good a hurtful activity as any. If the company is seen as unjust, and the workers know, as they do, that the company wants production, then they may find that withholding production is the most satisfactory of revenges. And of course it will hurt the foreman's record.

You may say that I have emphasized material rewards, promotion and pay, when much more powerful rewards for many men are achievement and the gaining of recognition for a good job done in taking responsibility.[11] So I have. But I have been talking about ordinary repetitive work. Not only is it hard to provide achievement rewards at this level, for the scope of responsibility is low, but the material rewards are more important at this level too: not until a man has a full belly (and a washing machine) can he find "higher" values particularly rewarding. At a higher level, the situation undoubtedly changes. Since a high-level supervisor can provide "higher" rewards, and he has a greater monopoly over their supply, it seems quite likely that the power that he has over his subordinates can be greater than that of a low-level one over *his*. If I had taken as the typical supervisor the president of a company, it would probably have been found that his behavior made more difference to the behavior of his immediate subordinates than the foreman's behavior makes to the behavior of manual workers.

CONCLUSION

In American industry the variations in production that may be attributed to the immediate activity of the workers, without changes in methods, machinery, or power, are large but not enormously large. They are small compared to the long-run increases

[11] See Frederick Herzberg, B. Mausner, and B. B. Snyderman, *The Motivation to Work* (New York: John Wiley and Sons, 1959).

brought about by capital investment in new technologies. The part of the variation that may be attributed to the behavior of foremen is on the average smaller still. The reason in both cases is, I think, that the factors making for increased production are located increasingly, not in any particular parts of the organization, but in the workings of the organization as a whole. The practical consequence is that the top management, which always made a difference, makes more difference than it used to. The more complicated the nervous system, the more important is the action of the brain.

3

Toward an Understanding of the Leadership Role in Formal Organization

FLOYD C. MANN

This chapter is essentially a progress report. As the wording of the title indicates, the ideas being reported are still in the process of being developed and tested against the reality of managerial and supervisory roles in different organizations. While I will present first the approach or conceptual framework that some of us[1] are using in thinking about the leadership role

[1] A number of colleagues have contributed to the development of this orientation toward organizational leadership or the bits of evidence that we now have supporting this approach. These include James K. Dent, L. Richard Hoffman, Lawrence K. Williams, Basil S. Georgopoulos, and Franklin W. Neff. Others contributing less directly but importantly to my general thinking in this area are John R. P. French, Jr., Robert L. Kahn, and Rensis Likert. John Erfurt has worked as a close associate in the analysis and testing of these ideas during the year since an earlier draft of this paper was given at the American Sociological Association meetings in Washington, D.C., 1962.

Financially this research has been supported by a series of contracts and grants from the Detroit Edison Company and the National Institutes of Health.

in formal organizations, and then go on to describe research findings regarding this way of thinking, I would like to underscore that the research findings have contributed a good deal more to our theory in this area than the other way around. Thus, while this statement of our present thinking and research will go from theory to findings, the findings are actually shaping the theory.

A CONCEPTUAL FRAMEWORK

THE ORGANIZATIONAL ROLE OF SUPERVISOR

To understand the role of supervisor, manager, administrator, or leader in a large, complex organization, it is necessary first to describe briefly some of the basic elements in the structure and functioning of these complex social systems. Using the primary concepts of organizational objective, task, office, and work group or "organizational family," I will identify the concept of the generic term *supervisor* as a basis for analyzing the nature of this essential organizational role.

An organization is designed to accomplish something: this is its *objective* or *purpose*. Given the objective, it is possible to plan a division of labor and thus bring into being a structure of *tasks* or *activities* that must be performed to accomplish an objective of an organization. A *task* is a set of individual behaviors which may involve tools or other physical or human objects directed toward a specific organizational objective. It is a *molar* unit of behavior that has a particular duration and setting. It is the most basic unit in the development of the concept of supervisor.

An *organizational office* is a set of tasks performed by a single individual. An office is the "building block" of the organization. Offices may in turn be grouped together to designate *work groups, departments,* and then *divisions* as units within succeedingly larger functional areas in the organization. The tasks that are done in separate offices have to be interrelated if the organization is to accomplish its objective. The greater the specialization, the greater the need for coordination among organizational offices.

This need brings into existence new tasks and activities of directing, controlling, and coordinating. The tasks within a small group of offices are interrelated and directed by the occupant of a superordinate office. For example, the first-line supervisor's primary job is to direct the activities of the occupant in offices under him (subordinates). The directing of the activities of these supervisors is in turn coordinated by the occupant of the next higher superordinate office (the department head), who has this as one of his primary tasks. The controlling activities of a group of department heads are in turn coordinated by occupants of the next higher echelon in the organization. A division of labor with its high specialization of tasks thus brings into existence a vertical structure of offices—key organizational offices whose occupants have as one of their primary tasks the supervision of the subordinates immediately under them.

A complex organization is made up of a large number of relatively small face-to-face *work groups* or *organizational families*. Each of these units has its own subobjective and sets of specialized tasks to perform. At the same time, the subobjectives and activities of each unit are a part of the total objective of the organization. By design, each of these work units is interlocked with other units through the activities of the generic office of *supervisor*. An organizational family then is defined as a group of offices occupied by a supervisor and his immediate subordinates in which is lodged the responsibility for meeting a subobjective of the organization by accomplishing particular tasks within the total division of labor.

Structurally, the organizational role of the supervisor at any level is primarily one of linking together different parts of the organizational structure of work groups and integrating the specialized performances of these units. This is the role on which the entire system depends to achieve and maintain unity and coherence. Specifically, at the structural level, the role of the supervisor entails the following functions: (1) directing and coordinating the tasks and activities of the subordinates within the supervisor's work group; (2) relating these activities to those of other work groups at the same organizational level within which his group interacts, and (3) relating the activities of his group and his own activities to those of other organizational units operating at the next higher, as well as the next lower level in the organization. The role of the supervisor may be viewed as that of a structural coordinative "linking pin," involving social psychological functions to coordinate individual member needs and goals with organizational objectives.

The *raison d'être* of every organization is to accomplish some objective. The physical and mental capacities and energies of men are among the principal means and resources through which the objectives of organizations can be attained. But men —the occupants of the organization's offices—also have their own goals which they want to attain while working in the organization. The interests of the individual members of the organization, and the goals which they are trying to attain, may or may not be the same as, or compatible with, those of the organization. The degree of congruence between the objectives of the organization and the goals of its members varies considerably among different types of organizations.

One of the basic problems of organizations, then, is how to reconcile, coordinate, or integrate member needs and goals with organizational requirements and objectives. This social psychological aspect of the role of the supervisor in the complex organization is of key importance; it is here that the supervisor must deal with the *motivational* problem of relating man and system.

The magnitude of this motivational-coordinative linking will vary directly according to the actual and potential discrepancy between organizational and individual goals. The discrepancy can be large or small. It can vary among organizations of different types, from one organizational level to another, within the same organization from one time to another as the organization moves from one stage of its development to another. There will probably be more congruence between the objectives of the organization and the goals of the members in voluntary organizations than in those based on a contractural relation between member and organization; there will probably be more congruence in the upper than in the lower echelons of the organization; and there will probably be more congruence early in the life of an organization than in its later stages.

What is meant by saying that the magnitude of this problem of coordinating these two sets of goals—the problem of motivation—varies markedly with the level of the organizational-supervisory role? The principal executive of an organization and the heads of major departments face virtually no motivation problem. These individuals have either established the objectives of the organization, and/or determined the means of attaining the objectives, or have been selected to fill these positions because their own personal needs and values were congruent with organizational aims. At the other extreme, the first-line supervisor is constantly confronted with the task of making organizational objectives compatible with the needs and goals of his subordinates. Intermediate levels of supervision also have to reconcile the two sets of goals but the problem becomes increasingly less severe at successively higher levels. It is the foreman who has the toughest job in this respect. He ordinarily has had the least to say about the objectives of the organization, but is expected to understand these objectives fully and to make them meaningful imperatives to those under his supervision. To handle creatively this motivational-coordinative linking of organizational objectives and subordinate needs and goals, the supervisor must know a great deal about the organization and the problems it faces and a great deal about immediate subordinates and the problems which each of them feel they face. It is the role of the supervisor to make meaningful the goals of each to the other and in the last analysis to coordinate these two systems of goals and needs. This task of interlocking personal needs and impersonal objectives frequently requires a very high order of creative and imaginative problem solving.

Thus, the role of the supervisor contains at least two important classes of coordinative functions: (1) those that are sociologically and structurally required if each subunit's objectives are to be made compatible by this office with the organization's over-all objective, and (2) those that are required social psychologically and motivationally if individual members' energies and goals and organizational objectives are to be interrelated. In general, the first class of structural coordinative functions have been most important and visible at the top of organizational systems, and the second class of motivational coordinative functions at the bottom or lower levels.

SUPERVISORY SKILLS

The preceding discussion of the concept of supervisor has direct implications concerning the essential skills that a supervisor must have. To perform the functions required to coordinate the activities of one organizational family with another, the supervisor must have *administrative competence*. To integrate organizational objectives with individual member needs, he must have *human-relations competence*. To accomplish his other assigned tasks, including the performance of technical operations, he must possess *technical competence*.

The marked division of labor and high degree of specialization that characterize large-scale organizations require that each supervisor have at least the minimum technical competence necessary to understand and direct the work being done within his organizational unit. The higher the degree of specialization and differentiation of activities, the greater the need for supervisors with technical competence in the tasks performed by the unit. *Technical skill,* or competence, as used here, refers to the ability to use pertinent knowledge, methods, techniques, and equipment necessary for the performance of specific tasks and activities, and for the direction of such performance. Fundamentally, it involves understanding and proficiency with respect to a specific class of functions in the organization. These include not only concrete motor skills, but also the abstract orientations and basic frames of reference that are normally associated with particular professional roles and affiliations. Technical skills may be acquired through formal training in professional schools, informal on-the-job training, or combinations of academic and internship or apprenticeship programs.

Just as technical skills are primarily concerned with task-centered competence, human-relations skills are concerned with the ability to work with other people effectively. In the case of supervisors, the other people involved are his subordinates, superiors, other supervisors at the same level, and occasionally staff specialists from other units within the organization. *Human-relations skills*, then, refer to the ability to use pertinent knowledge and methods for working with people and through people. They include an understanding of general principles of human behavior, particularly those principles which involve the regulation of interpersonal relations and human motivation, and the skillful utilization of this understanding in day-to-day interaction with others in the work situation.

The supervisor with human-relations skills understands how the principles of behavior affect not only others but himself as well. He knows how both his own and others' frames of reference color what is perceived and assumed to be reality, how attitudes, beliefs, opinions, and values affect behavior and learning, and how needs and aspirations shape an individual's investment of his energies. Included in these skills is the ability to represent the needs and goals of members at different levels in the organization to each other so that each can comprehend the problems faced by the other. Central to human-relations skills is the ability of the supervisor to integrate the goals of individuals with the objectives of the organization. The supervisor must be able to identify those needs of others which are central to their self concept, and to relate these to organizational objectives in a manner that is psychologically meaningful and rewarding to them. At times this requirement will mean simply coordinating the goals of one's subordinates with those of people in higher levels; at other times, it will mean creating, modifying, or shifting either organizational objectives or individual goals so that an operational congruence or integration between the two can be attained. Basically, the present class of skills involves managing the emotional and motivational dimensions of interpersonal relations in an organization.

The third class of basic supervisory skills deals with administrative competence. *Administrative skill* or competence, refers to the ability of the supervisor to think and act in terms of the total system within which he operates—in terms of the organization as a system of people and physical objects, with its own image, structure, and process, which functions as a continuing complex problem-solving arrangement to attain particular objectives. The emphasis here is on understanding and acting according to the objectives of the total organizational system, rather than on the basis of the goals and needs of one's immediate work group. Administrative skills include planning, programing, and organizing the work; assigning the right tasks to the right people; giving people the right amount of responsibility and authority; inspecting and following up on the work; and coordinating the efforts and activities of different organizational members, levels, and departments. In short, administrative skill requires an ability to conceptualize and comprehend the organizational system as a whole, and to act in terms of this over-all organizational framework.

To summarize briefly, there are three classes of skills which supervisors need to perform in their key role in the formal organization—technical skills, human-relations skills, and administrative skills. Technical skills pertain to "know-how" competence regarding particular tasks or activities for which the supervisor is responsible. Human-relations skills concern the understanding of organization members as people with their own problems and needs, and the understanding of the emotional and motivational dimensions of interpersonal relations. Administrative skills deal with the coordinative and integrative activities required for the attainment of the objectives of the total organizational system. Thus, the three kinds of skills concern tasks, people, and organization, respectively.

THE SUPERVISORY SKILL MIX

While all supervisors must have some minimum technical skill, some minimum human-relations skill, and some minimum administrative skill, the mix of these skills will vary by organizational level and through the history of an organization. What is an effective combination of skills for supervisors at one organizational level may not be an effective skill mix for supervisors at another level. What is an effective combination at one time in the life of an organization may not be an effective combination at a later period.

Considering first the relativity of this skill mix by levels, we might expect that at the lower levels of an organization, the technical and human-relations skills would be the most important. At the intermediate levels, technical skills may be less important and administrative skills more important. And at the top-management and executive levels, administrative skills would be the most important. Human-relation skills are probably important for supervisors at all levels, but, in view of the earlier suggestion that the motivation problem is not as acute at the higher levels, human-relations skills are likely to be comparatively less important as one moves up the hierarchy. Certainly, there are no substitutes for either administrative competence at the top or technical competence at the bottom levels of the organization.

In addition to the variations in skill mix required at different organizational levels, there is probably a good deal of variation in the skill requirements at different times. Early in the life of an organization, technical and human-relations skills are probably essential; later, as the organization becomes more complex, administrative skills become increasingly crucial. Similarly, during periods of rapid change, technical skills are likely to become very important. With the initiation of a reorganization, or when a new technology is introduced in the system, upper-level supervisory personnel have to draw more heavily on their technical competence at the early stages. During such a period of transition, the problems faced by the organization are basically of a technical character, and their solution depends very greatly on a thorough command of specialized knowledge and technical-analytical ability. But, in the latter stages of reorganization and change, human-relations skills assume greater importance once again; after the technical difficulties have been overcome, the remaining organizational problems are frequently of the human-relations variety. Thus, it is not enough to think in terms of the combination of the three kinds of supervisory skills required at different organizational levels. It is also necessary to consider the time dimension—how their combination, for a particular level, must vary over time.

THE RELATIVITY OF "EFFECTIVE" SUPERVISION

This approach to the leadership role in the formal organization underscores the relativity of supervision. It adds to the complexity of the problem of conceptualization and measurement, but simultaneously reassures in that it appears to be more consistent and meaningful in terms of actual experience of supervisors and administrators at all levels, and consistent with research findings in the field. The problem is to identify the mixtures and combinations of the several classes of skills that are most appropriate in given organizations, for given organizational levels, and at given times. This problem is not easy, but it is researchable. Bits and pieces from a number of different field studies have brought research to this point in understanding what constitutes effective leadership. Perhaps this framework will provide a more useful model on which to build and test.[2]

---

[2] It is not an objective of this chapter to relate this conceptual framework to other theories of the leadership role. This is being done as a part of another publication.

RESEARCH FINDINGS

As was indicated at the outset, the preceding ideas represent a current formulation of the complex role of leadership in formal organization. This conceptualization has been an outgrowth of empirical research findings in the programs of Organizational Behavior and Change in the Survey Research Center at the University of Michigan. Now to consider these findings.

EARLY PROGRAM FINDINGS: PRODUCTIVITY STUDIES

Early in our research we did a series of studies investigating the relationship between leadership and group performance. Kahn and Katz[3] summarized the bits and pieces of information from those several studies concerning the performance of a variety of work groups and the characteristics of each group's supervisor. Using the specific findings from studies in the clerical offices of an insurance company, section gangs on a railroad, and workers in a tractor factory, they concluded that there were four classes of leadership-relevant variables which appeared to be consistently related to the productivity of an organization and the psychological returns which the group offers its members. In essence, the findings were as follows:

1. Supervisors of more effective groups were better able to play a differentiated role than the supervisors of the less effective groups. This point Kahn and Katz derived from specific findings which indicated the better supervisors spent more time in planning what was to be done, in providing necessary materials, and in actual supervision rather than in straight production work.

2. The better supervisors delegated authority to others more than the poorer supervisors. This point was derived from find-

---

[3] Robert L. Kahn and Daniel Katz, "Leadership Practices in Relation to Productivity and Morale." In Dorwin Cartwright and Alvin Zander (eds.), *Group Dynamics: Research and Theory* (Evanston, Illinois: Row, Peterson and Company, 1953), pp. 612-627.

ings showing that the better supervisors did not supervise as closely, gave less detailed work instructions, and gave subordinates greater freedom in planning their jobs and setting their own work pace.

3. The more effective supervisors were more supportive in their relationships with their subordinates and gave more attention to creating employee motivation. This finding concerning the employee orientation of the better supervisor was based on a great number of specific relationships about how the better supervisor took a personal interest in the employee as a whole person, was more understanding and less punitive when mistakes were made, was concerned with the training and development of his men, and generally maintained a more open system of communication between himself and his men.

4. The supervisors of the more effective groups had work groups which had developed greater cohesiveness among members of the group than those groups which were doing a less effective job. This point was based on specific findings indicating that productivity was related to how good a job employees felt their units were doing in comparison to others, and in the extent to which employees felt identified with their group and felt they were "really a part of their group."

The first two classes of variables—stressing the supervisor's abilities to play a differentiated role and to delegate—pointed to specific components of the supervisor's "administrative skills." Kahn and Katz recognized this relationship in their interpretation of how the differentiated role of the supervisor affected productivity of the group. They felt that attention given to planning, including the coordination and organization of the tasks of the group, had a direct effect upon output. They even spoke of this as a type of engineering or institutional skill in which the technical know-how of the supervisor is brought to bear upon the ordering of the work of the group on a long-range basis. Their third grouping of variables—the supportive, employee-oriented quality of the relationship between the supervisor and his subordinates—is similar with what are now called human-relations skills.

In retrospect it is now possible to see why our early field research could not have distinguished very clearly among different classes of supervisory skills. For one thing, at that time we were focusing on the human-relations component of the subordinate-superior relationship. For another, we were studying problems of the foreman and first-line supervisors at the very lowest levels of organization where the human-relations skills of the superior were highly visible in affecting unit performance. We had not yet had many opportunities to look intensely at the skills required of occupants of departmental and top-level executive offices where administrative skills should predominate. And much of our early research dealt with the problems of the supervisor of highly engineered assembly lines of either white- or blue-collar workers where there was little need for first-line supervisors or foremen to have administrative and coordinative skills. It is noteworthy that the specific findings regarding the importance of planning, providing materials for the men, and figuring work out ahead of time came from the railroad study where there were no routinized or machine-dictated work technologies.

EARLY PROGRAM FINDINGS: APPRAISALS OF SUPERIORS

Another early study which I feel contributed markedly to the development of this present conceptualization of a trilogy of supervisory competences was one relating the *Appraisals of Superiors and Attitudes of Their Employees.*[4] This study, conducted in eight accounting departments of an electric-power company, allowed us to compare the summary appraisal ratings made by department heads of first-line supervisors with subordinate's perceptions of and attitudes toward these supervisors.

Each supervisor's appraisal was prepared in writing and

[4] Floyd C. Mann and James K. Dent, *Appraisals of Supervisors and Attitudes of Their Employees in an Electric Power Company* (Ann Arbor: Survey Research Center, 1954).

agreed to unanimously by four department heads (one of whom was the supervisor's immediate superior) after there had been a discussion of the supervisor and his work. In this appraisal conference the supervisor was given one of six evaluations ranging from "Immediately Promotable" to "Unsatisfactory." As a part of another study, we asked the employees under these supervisors to fill out a lengthy questionnaire about their perceptions and satisfactions in the work situation. Most of the questions regarding the supervisor dealt with his human-relations skills.

We then analyzed these two bodies of data to see the extent of agreement between the evaluations made of first-line superiors by their department heads and the "evaluations" made of these same superiors by the employees in their work groups. The findings indicated that there was a good deal of agreement in these evaluations for the very effective and the least effective supervisors. For a few of the questions asked of the employees, like "How free do you feel to discuss personal problems with your superior," there was a direct and orderly relationship between the per cent who answered "very free" and the appraisal classification given these supervisors by their department heads. To be specific, 54 per cent of the employees under supervisors rated "Immediately Promotable" said they felt "very free" to discuss personal problems with their supervisor, 44 per cent of those under "Promotable" supervisors said this, as did 34 per cent under those rated "Satisfactory Plus," 30 per cent under those appraised as "Satisfactory," 27 per cent under those rated by management as "Questionable," and only 19 per cent of the employees under the supervisors rated as "Unsatisfactory" said they felt "very free" to discuss personal problems with their supervisor.

For many questions, like the general summary question of "How good is your supervisor in handling people," this relationship was not so clear-cut. Employees under "Promotable" supervisors frequently gave a less favorable (though not statistically significant) report than the employees under "Satisfactory Plus." One day, after we had found that we could not explain this discontinuity by any of the other variables we had measured in the study, we were discussing this anomaly with the company's general accountant. He said without hesitation, "I can probably give you a lead to that. That 'Promotable' group is comprised of supervisors who are accountants and actuaries, technically very competent and whom we expect to promote to higher jobs later after they have learned to deal with people better. The 'Satisfactory Plus' group, on the other hand, are very skilled in dealing with employees, but do not yet have the technical and professional training required for promotion to the next level of jobs here where specialized knowledge is so important." The implications of this discussion for recognizing the technical component of a supervisor's role are obvious.

These findings, together with a brief experience with John R. P. French, Jr., and Clayton Hill in teaching graduate students in a business-school course about the difference between man-to-man, man-to-small-group, and man-to-total-organization skills, combined to emphasize the importance of investigating more systematically the technical, human-relations, and administrative skills as distinct classes.

THE STUDY OF SUPERVISION IN TWO POWER PLANTS

The first opportunity that occurred to use this new orientation was in a study of two power plants as prototypes of the more automated plants of the future.[5] Among other questions concerning foreman practices, the power-plant workers were asked to evaluate their foremen on the three dimensions of competence. After a good deal of exploratory interviewing to identify more specifically the kinds of knowledge or behavior being considered, we wrote, pretested, and used three questions as a part of a large battery of items about different aspects of the jobs. These questions were:

[5] Floyd C. Mann and L. Richard Hoffman, *Automation and the Worker: A Study of Social Change in Power Plants* (New York: Henry Holt and Company, 1960).

How well does your foreman know the technical side of his job—the
operation and maintenance of the equipment for which he is
responsible?

How well does your foreman do the administrative side of his job—
by this we mean planning and scheduling the work, indicating
clearly when work is to be finished, assigning the right job to the
right man, inspecting and following up on the work that is done,
etc.?

How well does your foreman do the human-relations side of his job—
getting people to work well together, getting individuals to do the
best they can, giving recognition for work done, letting people
know where they stand, etc.?

For each of these questions the respondents were asked to answer in terms of one of five alternatives varying from "He han-
dles these parts of his job extremely well" through "Fairly Well"
to "Does not handle these parts of his job at all well."

The first question we wanted to answer was whether the
respondents were able to differentiate among the three areas of
competence. Zero-order product-moment correlations ranged
from .5 correlations between technical and human-relations
skills in the two plants to .7 correlations between administrative
and human-relations skills. These suggested that the nonsupervisory men were distinguishing most clearly between technical
and human-relations skills of their supervisors and least between
administrative and human-relations skills. Partial correlations between each of the pairs of skills holding the third constant con-
firmed this suggestion. The partial correlations between technical and human-relations skills for the two plants were .2 and .1
and were significantly lower than the other two corresponding partial correlations. The partials between administrative and
human-relations skills were .56 for both plants; the partials for
technical and administrative skills of the order of .4.

After having established that the men in these plants were
distinguishing most clearly between the technical and human-
relations skills of their supervisors, the second question we wanted

to answer was which of these classes of skills were most important. Since these two plants were highly integrated systems and
moreover one of them was new and more automated technologically than the other, we found we could not obtain any comparable "hard criteria"—like operating or efficiency statistics—*by
work groups* to assess the importance of the different supervisory
skills. The one criterion of supervisory effectiveness which was
available to us was the satisfaction of the men with their immediate supervisors. As a part of our battery of questions, each man
had been asked, "Taking all things into consideration, how satisfied are you with your immediate supervisor." We used this
criterion.

Zero-order correlations between the worker's perceptions of
his supervisor's competencies and the worker's over-all satisfaction with his supervisor ranged from the upper fifties to .76.
Again the story was in the partial correlations. When each of the
supervisory skills was correlated with satisfaction, holding the
effect of the other skills constant, we found that the men's perceptions of their foreman's human-relations skills were most
strongly associated with their satisfaction. In both plants, the
partial correlation between perceived human-relations competence and employee satisfaction with supervisor was significantly
greater than the partial correlation between the perceived technical competence and employee satisfaction. The criterion of employee satisfaction with supervisors being the measure of effectiveness, the most important function of the supervisor was
his ability to deal with his subordinates as human beings rather
than his ability to handle technical equipment. And the relative
importance of these two factors seemed to be the same for the
supervisors in both the more automated and the older plant.

In addition to the trilogy questions, our questionnaire asked
for information about how the men saw or evaluated their foremen in terms of 30 other supervisory behaviors. Some specific
questions dealt with bits of behavior that are characteristic of a
supervisor who is competent in human-relations skills—how con-

siderate he is of men's feelings, whether he recognizes good work by praising sincerely and thoroughly, and the like. Other items could be characteristic of supervisors who were competent in both technical and human-relations skills, or perhaps only in technical skills, or in neither.

Since the men had been least clear in distinguishing administrative from human-relations and technical skills, we decided to see whether the men saw these specific supervisory behaviors as primarily related to the human-relations or technical competence of their supervisor. Partial correlations, partialing out the effects first of human-relations and then of technical competence, showed that 13 of our specific supervisory-behavior items were primarily associated with the men's perception of their supervisor's human-relations skills. Taken as a whole, these items suggested that the foreman with whom employees were most satisfied was the one who considered them as individuals, both in his relations to them on the job and in seeing that they got ahead in the organization.

A second group of five specific supervisory behaviors, related to both human-relations and technical competence, suggested that some supervisory behaviors serve a dual function. As a class, these appeared to be task-facilitating behaviors. However, they required the foreman to display a certain degree of understanding for the worker as a man, as well as knowledge about the technical aspects of the job. Our hypothesis was these would be most highly related to a criterion of productivity—if we had had one. Our assumption was that productivity would be furthered by a foreman's consideration of his employees in the way he imparted his technical knowledge to them.

The remainder of the specific supervisory behaviors were unrelated to either the foreman's technical or human-relations competence or were not consistently related to one or the other of these two competences. This analysis of specific behaviors indicated that our research had been focused primarily on the human-relations skills of the supervisory role.

In summary, this first study using the trilogy of supervisory skills indicated that (1) nonsupervisory men in power plants were distinguishing most clearly between the technical and human-relations skills of their superiors, (2) the men's overall satisfaction with their supervisors was primarily related to their perceptions of his human-relations skills, and (3) our questions about the specific behaviors of supervisors were focused primarily on the human-relations dimension of the leadership role.

SUPERVISION AT DIFFERENT LEVELS IN
COMMUNITY GENERAL HOSPITALS

The next opportunity we had to contribute empirically to the building of our conceptual framework regarding the role of supervisor came when we undertook a study of administrative problems in the community general hospital.[6] In our study of ten short-stay hospitals with from 100 to 350 beds, the set of three questions regarding supervisory competences was asked of five groups of respondents in each hospital: administrative-department heads, supervisory nurses, nonsupervisory registered nurses, practical nurses, and laboratory and X-ray technicians. As in the power-plant study, the respondents were asked first to indicate the name of their *immediate supervisor*, and then to answer the trilogy questions along with others about how they saw this person's supervision.

Simple analyses, comparing the ten hospitals with the power plants, indicated that all groups of respondents in the hospitals perceived their supervisors as handling the three supervisory skills better than the men in the power plants saw their foremen handling them. Moreover, every group in the hospital evaluated its supervisors highest on technical skill, next highest on administrative skill, and lowest on human-relations skill. There

---

[6] Basil S. Georgopoulos and Floyd C. Mann, *The Community General Hospital* (New York: The Macmillan Company, 1962).

had been no clear ordering relationship among these three in the first study.

The findings from the nonsupervisory registered nurses in the ten hospitals combined are illustrative of the pattern of responses found in the answers from the other groups and levels in the hospital. Of these nurses, 81 per cent perceived their immediate supervisor as handling the technical role of the job extremely well or very well, 72 per cent as handling the administrative side equally well, and 68 per cent perceived the supervisor as handling the human-relations side equally well. The differences among the groups in how highly they evaluated their supervisor's skills were not very great, except that the technicians in the laboratories and in X-ray were a good deal more critical about the administrative and human-relations skills of their immediate superiors.

Having established that the occupants of the supervisory offices in these ten hospitals were generally seen by subordinates as strongest in technical skill and weakest in human-relations skill, we then looked at the question of how interrelated the three skills were. Simple rank-order correlations across the hospitals showed that the three skills were highly and significantly related to one another, with only an occasional exception. In general these simple correlations, using hospitals rather than individuals as the unit of analysis, showed that technical and human-relations skills were the least closely related and technical and administrative skills were the most closely related. The correlation between administrative and human-relations skills occupied an intermediate position.

Of particular importance in the development of our theoretical thinking was the fact that we found the relationship among the three skills tending to vary from one level of supervision to another. From both simple rank-order and simple tau correlations, the three skills were found most highly interrelated in the data from the practical nurses, and the least highly related when in the data from the technicians and department heads about their supervisors. Looking at the relationship among the three skills based on data from the three nursing groups, we found that the relationship between technical and human-relations skills decreased as we moved up the hierarchy from practical, through registered, to supervisory nurses, and the same trend tended to hold for the relationship between technical and administrative skills.

We then investigated how clearly each of the three skills is distinguished in the hospital as an organization. In spite of the limitations of a population of only ten hospitals we computed partial tau correlations among the three supervisory skills for each group. While partial rho correlations cannot be computed with an N as small as ten, partial taus can. There are no tests of significance for the latter. The findings from this computation indicated that:

1. When the effects of administrative skill are held constant, the relationship between technical and human relations skills in the ten hospitals is very small for each supervisory level. The partial tau for the department heads was .15; for the technicians, .01; for the supervisory nurses, .07; and .33 and .30 for the registered and practical nurses, respectively.

2. When the effects of technical skill are eliminated, the relationship between human-relations and administrative skills is small to moderate—ranging from .15 for department heads to .51 for supervisory nurses.

3. When the effects of human-relations skills are removed, the relationship between technical and administrative skills is moderate to high, ranging from .42 to .72.

By level or group, the partial taus suggest that:

1. Department heads most clearly distinguish between technical and human-relations skills and between human-relations and administrative skills, and the least between technical and administrative skills.

2. Laboratory and X-ray technicians and supervisory nurses distinguish the most clearly between technical and human-relations skills.
3. The nonsupervisory registered nurses distinguish most clearly between the human-relation and administrative skills of their superiors.
4. As in the case of the simple correlational analyses, the practical nurses were the least discriminating of the five groups. However, their greatest discrimination was between technical and human-relations skills.

As in the power-plant study, the next question we wanted to ascertain was how each of these three skills of supervisory personnel in the hospitals related to the satisfaction of subordinates with supervision. Again we used a summary question regarding satisfaction with the immediate supervisor: "Taking all things into consideration, how satisfied are you with your immediate supervisor?" As might be expected, simple correlations indicated that each of the three skills was positively and significantly related to the satisfaction of subordinates with their supervisors. This finding held for all groups except the practical nurses—the group that distinguished least well among these skills. Again the story was in the partial correlations, and again we had to use partial taus because of the small number of organizations being used.

The findings from this analysis indicated that when the effects of the second and third skills are partialed out statistically:

1. Technicians' satisfactions with their supervisors is primarily associated with the technicians' perceptions of the supervisor's technical (.54) and human-relations skills (.56).
2. Supervisory nurses' satisfaction with their immediate supervisors is primarily related to their perception of their supervisor's human relations skills (.71).
3. Department heads' satisfaction with their immediate su-

pervisor (the administrator) is primarily related to their perception of his administrative skill (.73).

For the other groups—the registered nurses and the practical nurses—satisfaction with the superior was not highly related to any one or combination of their supervisor's skills in dealing with the tasks, the people, or the organization.

The most important findings here, in terms of our framework regarding the role of the supervisor in formal organization, were that technical and human-relations skills of the supervisor tended to be the most highly related to satisfaction with the supervisor for the lower-level laboratory and X-ray groups, and administrative skills (with human-relations skills only a poor second) were primarily related to satisfaction for the top-level group in the hospital—the department heads.

In summary then, the findings from five different groups and several different levels in the hospital study suggested that the mix of supervisory skills varied by level and that different skills or skill mixes were related to our satisfaction-with-the-supervisor criterion.

SUPERVISION DURING A CHANGEOVER TO ELECTRONIC
DATA-PROCESSING EQUIPMENT

Observations and measures taken during a study of the organizational turmoil involved in a changeover to electronic data-processing equipment gave us a chance to contribute another dimension to our thinking about the role of the supervisor.[7, 8] This was the dimension of time. As we observed over a period of four years the problems faced by the different levels of supervisors

---

[7] Floyd C. Mann and Lawrence K. Williams, "Organizational Impact of the White Collar Automation," in *Proceedings of Eleventh Annual Meeting of Industrial Relations Research Association*, Chicago, December, 1958. Publication 22, 1959, pp. 55-69.

[8] Floyd C. Mann and Lawrence K. Williams, "Observations on the Dynamics of a Change to Electronic Data Processing Equipment," *Administrative Science Quarterly*, 5:217-256 (September, 1960).

in the accounting department of a large electric company in the course of directing the major reorganization required for the transition from equipment of the IBM 400 series through 650's to a 705, we came to feel that superiors had to be able to draw upon various combinations of skills at different times. During such a long period of change, different combinations of the three skills appeared to be required at different levels in the organization at the same time, and of the same supervisors at different times. In general, there seemed to be an initial shift in emphasis from human-relations to technical and administrative skill, and back again to human-relations skills at the end of the transition period.

When the organization was relatively stable before the changeover started, the supervisors seemed then to be drawing heavily upon their abilities that insured maintenance of the organization and of effective human relations. By contrast, the transitional period placed heavy demands on the supervisors' technical and cognitive skills. The problems of the transition period were basically technical and administrative, and only these kinds of skill and knowledge could solve them. Human-relations skills were not unimportant, but the job of laying out operationally feasible plans for complex changes in the accounting systems demanded competences other than human-relations skills. Superiors without adequate resources in all three skill components found their jobs extremely difficult during the transition.

As we followed the change through successive periods of the changeover, we felt that we could discern the movement of demand for different types of skills from one level to another in an organization. For example, with the announcement of the general plan to change to electronic data processing, the top levels of the management were primarily concerned with how to begin to implement the change administratively and technically, while the lower levels were concerned with allaying the fears that employees had regarding what the change held for them.

As the upper levels laid out general objectives for handling the change administratively and began to get the intermediate and lower levels of supervision involved in translating and implementing these changes into the technical work flows of the system, human-relations problems which could not be fully handled at the lower levels moved up to the top echelons for policy determination. And so on almost cyclically.

While this type of insight into the effect of different temporal situational demands on the skill mix of the effective supervisor came from our anthropological observations of the organization, we were not content to leave it at that. Therefore, in the battery of questionnaire items that we gave to this population of employees as aftermeasures on this natural field experiment, we asked the personnel to answer the following question:

Thinking back on your experience during the changeover, which one of the following supervisory qualities was most important to you at the time?

It was most important during the changeover that my supervisor: (*check one*)

1. Consult our group whenever there was a common problem
2. Plan and schedule work of our group
3. Be able to "iron out" the technical snags our group was having trouble with
4. Understand each of the jobs in our group
5. Listen to the problems that I and others in our group had

Of these five alternatives, the first and last were designed to measure human-relations skills, the third and fourth suggested technical skills, and the second related to administrative skill. Since we had only one alternative regarding the administrative-skill area, we focused our attention in this analysis on the human-relations and technical skills of the supervisors. The responses of employees in each work group were looked at separately and categorized as to whether the employees considered technical or human-relations skills to be the most important. The work groups were then divided into three classes:

a. Those centrally involved in the change
b. Those marginally involved in the change
c. Those which were essentially unaffected by the change to electric data processing

In the major-change work groups the technical skill of the supervisor was the most important; in the nonchange work groups, human-relations skills were found to be the most important. Of the 22 groups most highly involved in the change, employees in 17 indicated that technical skills were the most important, employees in only 5 groups said that human-relations skills were the most important. Of the 12 groups that were only marginally involved in the change, one half identified technical skills as the most important, the other half human-relations skills. Of the 12 groups which were not involved in the changeover, 8 stated that human-relations skills were the most important, 4 that technical skills were the most important. Statistical tests indicated that these differences were significant beyond the .05 level.

While these findings based on measures taken after the changeover could not demonstrate the cyclical way in which different supervisory skills appeared to be required at different times in the conversion, they do provide some confirmation that different skills are needed at different times. In those areas where the tasks were highly ambiguous and unstructured, there was apparently a greater demand for technical competence on the part of the supervisors. In the nonchange groups, by contrast, the human-relations skills were the most important.

Parenthetically it is interesting to note that within the major-change work groups four of the five units that indicated the human-relations skills were most important also described their supervisor as highly inefficient at human relations. The mean index score for human-relations skill in this group of supervisors was definitely lower than that for the remaining supervisors in the major-change work groups. This difference approached but did not reach statistical significance. This partial finding indicates that one of these three skills will predominate at any given time in an organization. Thus while technical skills were perhaps highly important for the individuals in these five groups, the fact that the supervisors were inadequate in human relations created problems which resulted in employees perceiving the human-relations ingredients as being highly necessary during the change.

To investigate further the importance of these different groups of skills at different times, we examined the relationship between employees' perceptions of their supervisor's technical and human-relations skills and the employees' over-all satisfaction with their immediate supervisor. Two groups of employees were identified: those whose jobs were highly influenced by the new electronic data-processing system and had thus been exposed to much change, and those whose jobs were not related to the new electronic data-processing system and had not been exposed to change. Findings from both groups indicated that employee satisfaction with their supervisor is more highly associated with their evaluation of his human-relations than his technical skill. However, satisfaction with the immediate supervisor was more strongly related to the evaluation of technical skills for the employees whose jobs were highly related to the new electric data-processing system than for the employees whose jobs were not changed. This finding provides further evidence of the greater importance of technical skills for supervisors in a period of change.

It was on the basis of these findings from observations, semi-structured interviews, and quantitative measures around the introduction of electronic data-processing equipment in the accounting departments that we began to see how the skill mix of a supervisor varied by time as well as by level in an organization.

SUPERVISION AT DIFFERENT STAGES IN THE LIFE CYCLE OF AN INDUSTRIAL PLANT

To extend further our understanding of this conceptual approach to leadership in formal organizations, we are currently studying the skill mix of supervisors at three different levels in six power plants which are arranged along a continuum from plants that are new or just being rebuilt to those that are almost technologically obsolete and about to be retired.

Using the same type of single-item questions regarding technical, human-relations, and administrative skills, we have found the following additional facts:

1. There is a direct relationship between level and the extent to which subordinates are able to distinguish between their supervisor's technical and human-relations skills. The higher the level, the sharper the distinction. (The correlation between technical and human-relations skills, with administrative skills partialed out, drops from .30 for nonsupervisory men to .23 for supervisors, and .10 for middle management.)

2. Men in new plants distinguish more sharply between their immediate supervisor's technical and human-relations skills than men in older plants. (Partial correlations are .17 and .16 in contrast to partial correlations in the upper thirties and lower forties.)

3. Foremen in new plants distinguish technical from administrative skills more clearly than foremen in older plants. (Partial correlations are .00 and .02 in new plants when human-relations skills are held constant statistically, in contrast to correlations in the fifties and seventies for foremen in older plants.)

4. The satisfaction of foremen with their supervisors in the new plants is more highly related to their perception of their immediate supervisor's administrative skills than his technical or human relations skills.

5. Foremen in the oldest plant are less able than foremen in other plants to distinguish between the technical, human-relations, and administrative skills of their immediate superiors in the front office.

6. In the oldest plant both the men's and the foremen's satisfaction with their immediate supervisors is more associated with their estimate of his human relations skills than with their estimate of his technical or administrative skills.

In sum, these findings suggest that it is in the new, more highly automated plants that men can distinguish most clearly between their foremen's technical and human-relations ˡskills, and that foremen can distinguish most clearly between their front-office superiors' technical and administrative skills. In the older plants—those about to be shut down, where there is little chance to demonstrate any but human-relations skills—foremen cannot distinguish among these three skills, and the satisfaction of both the foremen and their men is most highly associated with the supervisor's skills in dealing with people as human beings. Thus, late in the life cycle of a plant it seems that human-relations skill becomes the most important element in the skill mix of supervision.

Recognizing the limitation of the single items in measuring supervisory competence in the three areas, the current study in power plants was also designed to allow us to construct multiple-item indices. Three levels of subordinates were asked not only the three summary measures but from 17 to 27 additional questions about the specific behavior and knowledge of their supervisors. The answers given by each level were subjected to factor analysis. Three factors were identified empirically—technical, human-relations, and administrative skill—and items specific to each dimension were combined into indices. The technical-skill index contained three items:

When one of the men at your level doesn't know how to do a job, how frequently does your immediate supervisor have the "job know-how" to explain how it is done?
How much does your supervisor know about doing each of the jobs in your area?
How much does your immediate supervisor know about the equipment you are responsible for?

The human-relations-skill index contained five items:

Do you feel that your supervisor will go to bat or stand up for you?
In solving the job problems, does your supervisor generally try to

get the ideas and opinions of you and the other people at your level?

How often does your immediate supervisor express appreciation for your work?

How free do you feel to discuss important things about your job with your supervisor?

How much help do you feel you get from your supervisor when you really need it?

The administrative-skill index was made up of three items:

How frequently is work time lost because your supervisor fails to do the proper scheduling and planning?

How frequently have you been assigned to do a job only to find that someone was also assigned to do the very same thing?

To what extent does your supervisor keep up to date on new policies, rules, and regulations?

Our findings indicate that the highest interitem correlations were found in the technical-skill area, with the human-relations-skill area second, and the administrative-skill area third. This indication held for all three levels of respondents. Correlations between our single-summary items and their respective indices indicate that each individual item regarding human-relations skills was more highly correlated with its corresponding multiple-item index score than items for either technical skill or administrative skill.

Having established more sensitive measures of the three supervisory skills, we are now turning to the investigation of how the skill mix of the supervisor, as perceived by his subordinates, is related to the supervisor's own report of his work-situation satisfactions, his worries, and his health complaints. The analyses that have dealt with the first-line supervisor may be discussed first. In the six power plants we found that there were about ninety work groups in which we could match the supervisor and his employees, and in which at least three or more of the men had given us evaluations of their supervisor's three skills. While our initial hope had been to divide the distribution for each skill into thirds—high, middle, and low—it was not possible with only ninety work groups to use such a highly complex design and still test the significance of our findings statistically. Drawing on our knowledge that nonsupervisory employees distinguish most clearly between their supervisor's technical and human-relations skills and are not as able to identify administrative skills, we have concentrated our first investigations at this level on the factors associated with different mixes of technical and human-relations skills. Five groups of first-line supervisors were established by dividing their men's evaluations of them on each of these two skill areas into thirds. Three of these groups have consistent ratings—the same rank in the two skill areas, that is, high in both, medium in both, or low in both; two of the groups are made up of supervisors with inconsistent ratings, that is, higher in technical than human-relations skills or higher in human-relations than in technical skills. The five patterns and the number of supervisors in each are shown below:

Skill-Mix Pattern	Number of Supervisors
High-high	20
Medium-medium	21
Low-low	10
Human relations higher than technical	16
Technical higher than human relations	21
Total	89

Analysis-of-variance tests showed that these groups did not differ significantly on such background characteristics as age, education, or length of service as a supervisor. Different groups did, however, differ markedly from one another with respect to how the foremen themselves saw their work situation, how satisfied they were with different aspects of it, what kinds of things these foremen were worrying about, and what they had to say about their own health complaints. It will not be possible to show within the limitations of this chapter how each of these groups differed from the other, but broad patterns of results can be given. Discussion will focus particularly on three of these key patterns.

The High-High Pattern

First-line supervisors evaluated by the men in their work groups as being high in both technical and human-relations skills are different from supervisors in one or another of the other groups in that:

They are less satisfied with their immediate supervisor—especially his administrative skills.

They are less satisfied in general with the men who are their superiors in the front office of the plant.

They have a higher evaluation of how well their work group does in comparison with other similar work groups in getting the job done.

They do not feel in the middle between the workers and top management.

They worry less that a problem might come up that they would not be able to handle.

And they worry less about their job mobility—about "failure to get ahead" or being "in a rut."

They have fewer health complaints in general. Specifically by their own report they are less troubled with insomnia and nervousness; cardiac awareness; gas, acid-stomach, and ulcer trouble; and stiffness and arthritis.

The Technical-Higher-than-Human-Relations Pattern

Supervisors evaluated by their subordinates as higher in technical than in human-relations skills are different from other supervisors in that:

They are generally less satisfied with their promotional opportunities, their present wages, the job itself, and the training they have had for their job.

But they are more satisfied with their superiors in the front office of the plant.

They are clearly distinguished as feeling in the middle between the workers and top management and being bothered by it.

They score high on a scale designed to measure propensity to take risks.

Their worries are mostly concerned with what they perceive to be their failure to get ahead and they feel in a rut.

They score high on measures of insomnia and nervousness and on cardiac awareness.

The Human-Relations-Higher-than-Technical Pattern

Supervisors perceived by their men as being more competent in human relations than in the technical dimensions of their jobs are different from other supervisors in that:

They are generally more satisfied with the training they have had for their job, their immediate supervisor—especially his administrative skills, the men who are their superiors in the front office of the plant—in all three skill areas; and how well their plant is managed in general.

They do not feel in the middle between the workers and top management.

They score low on our measure of risk-taking propensity.

They worry about their job performance: whether they can do what is expected of them, whether they can handle a problem that might come up, about how good a job they are doing.

They worry more often about the possibility of losing their job.

They also complain more frequently about certain aspects of their health, particularly insomnia and nervousness, stiffness and arthritis. In this latter respect—stiffness and arthritis—they are markedly different from other groups.

The Other Two Congruent Patterns:
Medium-Medium and Low-Low

The supervisors evaluated as having technical and human-relations skills within the middle third of the distributions for these skills were not markedly different from other groups of supervisors. They are more satisfied with their present wages, worry less than others about the kind of a job they are doing or about losing their job, and generally have a lower evaluation of how good their work group is in getting the job done. In other respects they are not different. The pattern of responses for the ten supervisors who were rated as low in both sets of skills suggests they are not at all satisfied with their wages, their training, or the men who are their superiors in the front office of their plant. They feel in the middle and under considerable pressure are often irritated and annoyed with the way things are going, and feel the men in their work group do not understand the problems a supervisor has to face. They do not report worrying about their job nor do they complain about their health. To find that this latter group (the low-lows) were not worried about their jobs and reported no health complaints was surprising. Two hypotheses are possible: (a) these ten men were unwilling to admit they had any worries or problems in this area, or (b) this small group of supervisors knew the company would tolerate their inadequacies until their retirement. Either or both of these possibilities may have been operative.

First-line supervisors with different combinations of technical and human-relations skills have distinctive feelings about aspects of their work situations, unique worries, and health complaints. This evidence suggests how essential it is to have the correct skill mix for a particular level in an organization. Supervisors evaluated by their men as being strong in both technical and human relations—probably the ideal mix for foremen at this level—felt less "in the middle" regarding problems between the workers and top management and were less bothered by being the linking pin between these two groups. They were less worried about their job performance and their mobility. They had fewer complaints about their health. Supervisors with something less than this ideal mix of technical and human-relations skills were having problems in one or several aspects of their work situation, were more likely to be worrying about things, or to be reporting trouble with their health. The few foremen who were seen as weak in both skill dimensions felt in the middle, under considerable pressure, and often irritated and annoyed at the way things were going. The foremen who were strong in technical and weak in human-relations skills felt most in the middle and were most bothered by it. They were worrying about their failure to get ahead and complained of insomnia-nervousness and some anxiety about the functioning of their heart. The foremen who were strong in human-relations and short on technical skills, while not indicating they felt in the middle between the worker and top management, were not better off than their counterparts who had the opposite combination of skills. They were clearly worrying about their job performance and were uneasy about losing their jobs as foremen. They reported they did not sleep well, were nervous and tense, and more often had stiffness or aching joints or muscles, and rheumatism or arthritis. Thus, it would appear that it costs an individual a good deal to try to fulfill the office of first-line supervisor in a power plant with anything less than a high-level of both technical and human-relations skills.

These data demonstrate the manner in which we are now using this conceptual approach to identify groups of supervisors at different levels of an organization with unique mixes of skills. We are investigating how these mixes are related to the supervisor's perceptions of his situation, attitudes toward various aspects of his job, and his own report of his physical and mental health. Similar analyses of the role of the second-line supervisor and of the key management offices in power plants are now under way.

SUMMARY

This chapter presents theory and data from an ongoing sequence of organizational field studies in which the role of supervisory and administrative behavior is being investigated. The sites have included power plants, community general hospitals, and accounting and clerical units. The emergent findings suggest the usefulness of conceptualizing the generic role of supervisor as the one who interlocks organizational families and interrelates organizational objectives and requirements with the needs, goals, and behaviors of the members of his unit. Three different classes of skills seem to be required of supervisors and managers: technical, human-relations, and administrative—skills concerned with tasks, people, and organizations, respectively. Findings indicate that leadership in the formal organization is a highly relative process, with different combinations of supervisory-leadership skills and practices being required at different levels of supervision in the same organization and at different times in the life of an organization.

4

Supervisors: Evolution of an Organizational Role

DELBERT C. MILLER

The title "supervisor" is a generic term covering more than
400 different names in the United States Census classification
of occupational titles,[1] including such titles as traffic supervisor,
mine pit boss, buck swamper, corral man, boom master, gang
leader, and route supervisor. Sometimes the term supervisor
has been used to refer to all persons who direct the work of others.[2] This broad usage occurs in trying to identify all members
of an organization who bear a management responsibility, as
when training officers seek to emphasize the human-relations
and administrative responsibilities which are functions shared
by all "supervisors." A broad definition encompassing all first-
line, middle, and top management does bring to focus the common elements in managerial functions and ideology. It is as useful for social scientists who wish to identify similar patterns as it
is for top managers who wish to inculcate loyalty and secure in-

---

[1] Bureau of the Census, *1960 Classified Index of Occupations and
Industries* (Washington, D.C.: U.S. Department of Commerce), pp.
39-45, 73-75.

[2] *Job Relations Training,* Training Within Industry (Washington,
D.C.: War Manpower Commission), June 1, 1944.

creased effectiveness in their entire managerial and supervisory staff.

In spite of all efforts to give it such broad meaning, the title still carries the traditional meaning of first-line supervisor. "The supervisor" in this chapter will refer to the person who is supposed to do the actual job of supervising employees. The employees may be professionals or unskilled workers. They may be engaged in producing goods or services. The supervisor is held directly responsible for these employees and must direct them in face-to-face contact. The reader who is used to looking at organization charts must not be confused by the alternate use of the terms foreman and supervisor. There has long been a blue-collar and white-collar segregation which has maintained a prestige differential between the supervisor of production as contrasted with the supervisor of service or commercial activities. For our purposes, "supervisor" will include such persons as foremen, office supervisors, university department heads, school principals, head nurses, and research-laboratory group chiefs.

THE FOREMAN AS THE HISTORIC SUPERVISOR

The foreman has been called both the most important and the least important member of management. In a mass-production society his leadership is vital to the process of supplying material wants. There are over 1,000,000 foremen in the United States today.[3] To millions of workers, he is the immediate boss —the one who really counts in assigning work and in creating the social climate of their work group. To an earlier generation who saw him as a feared but respected figure, he was the colorful Bull of the Woods. To the social scientist, the foreman's position is a significant index to the internal forces of organization which are becoming general to all supervisory positions.

The position of foreman has felt the brunt of both mass-production technological advances and organizational changes

---

[3] Bureau of the Census, *Current Population Reports,* Labor Force, Series P-57, No. 200 (Washington, D.C.: March 1959), p. 16.

emerging in large-scale bureaucracies. The performance of the foreman and that of his workers is measurable. Industrial production is more measurable than other types of labor. The units produced, the cost of items, and the quantity of scrap can all be counted. The measurement of performance increases the foreman's insecurity. The fact that his position may be short-circuited makes the position even more insecure. If the foreman just had to report to his boss, he could cover up and report only favorable things—as, it seems, everyone else does. However, many staff people can report the foreman's activities to his boss and higher management. The union can and does go over his head. So do inspection, cost-control, engineering, and other staff departments. Down to the foreman comes the question, "Why didn't you inform us?" Down come commands to cooperate with staff people. Down come new people and new studies of his workers' performance. A foreman's life is not a happy one.

The foreman in the historic perspective of the last half century has been compelled to make five major accommodations. These are the (1) ideological accommodation, (2) engineering accommodation, (3) personnel accommodation, (4) organizational-systems accommodation, and (5) labor-relations accommodation.

IDEOLOGICAL ACCOMMODATION

The newly assigned foreman of fifty years ago was often a man who had won his place by a demonstration of hard work and skilled competence. He was a man who had worked many years on the bench. His advancement to the position of foreman was won by promotion within the ranks. Often he was merely told to "take charge." He knew what this meant because he had worked for other foremen and he followed their example. The ideological commitment to represent management was a stern requirement in the days when labor unions were regarded as conspiracies. The foreman's responsibilities for production and discipline required a strong-willed man. Even today, the commitment represents a marked adjustment in work and social role. As one foreman commented:

> You can't treat the men as equals. They take advantage of good treatment. When I used to be a man on the line, I knew the way I'd like to be treated if I were to be happy on the job. When I got to be foreman, I started to treat my men in the same way—in other words, the way I'd like to be treated—but you just can't do it. You can't change overnight what's been going on for 15 years, and these men have just been spoiled by not having too good supervisors in the past. They can always quit if they don't like the job.[4]

The new foreman must weigh his behavior in terms of its effect on his men's respect and on his ability to secure discipline and cooperation. He must neither commit the sin of officiousness nor the folly of fraternity. If he has his beer with the men after work, he must be judicious. When his wife visits with other wives of the men in her husband's department, she must learn that she is now the foreman's wife, and what she says about people in the plant will be repeated with authority. Most managements urge their new foremen and their wives to identify with a new social circle of foremen and their wives. The old social ties are to be cut slowly but surely, with informal friendships replaced by more formal contacts. On the job, the logics of cost and efficiency become guides to supervisory behavior, and when thoroughly inculcated mark the transition of the worker to foreman. His main function is to insure that the production or service schedules established for him are actually fulfilled. While performing this job, our foreman of 50 years ago handled such contributory functions as hiring, transferring, and firing men, training new people, planning the production schedule, finding ways of improving machines and production, dealing with complaints, absences, and lateness, inspecting the product, and working to improve quality. He would commonly step into

---

[4] F. J. Jasinski, "Human Relations Training: The Missing Link," *Personnel*, May 1956, p. 514.

the line or up to the bench to work on production or repair a machine tool. In the evening he might call at the home or at the hospital and chat with a worker who was ill. These functions were almost autonomous. The foreman was in charge and he made the decisions. He was a skilled worker, clothed with some latitude of decision-making authority.

ENGINEERING ACCOMMODATION

The first major development to alter the foreman's job was the growth of engineering departments. Engineering became both a research development and an engineering-improvement division. The foreman was given instructions as to what machines he was to have, how they were to be placed, how he was to operate them, and how they were to be cared for. He was told he must go by the blueprints even when his judgment told him that there was a better way to proceed. Sometimes he could have his say but usually the engineers had their way. When time-and-motion engineers were sent into the shop, the foreman was asked to give the men a pep talk about cooperation while the engineers set production quotas and the amount of time the worker could have in the toilet. When piece-rate incentives were introduced, foremen were asked to push their groups into line with the pace setters.

The inventor of techniques of time-and-motion study, Frederick W. Taylor, once testified what this role had meant when he was the foreman of a work group operating his system:

I was a young man in years, but I give you my word I was a great deal older than I am now, what with the worry, meanness, and contemptibleness of the whole damn thing. It is a horrid life for any man to live, not to be able to look any workman in the face all day long without seeing hostility there, and feeling that every man around you is your virtual enemy. These men were a nice lot of fellows, and many of them were my friends outside the works. This life was a miserable one and I made up my mind to either get out of the business entirely and go into some other line of work, or to find some remedy for this unbearable condition.[5]

To this day the foreman's most bitter rival is the engineer. He sees himself pitting his hard earned plant knowledge of technical skill against the college textbook knowledge of the engineers. The foreman likes to catch engineers suggesting some foolish or less efficient method which they have devised in ignorance of better traditional techniques. It is usually an uneven contest and the foreman must make the accommodation.

PERSONNEL ACCOMMODATION

When a personnel department is established, it usually begins as an employment office. Prospective employees are screened and although office supervisors often make the decision as to whom they shall hire, the plant foreman is usually told to put to work the new employees which the personnel department has hired. It is explained to the foreman that this arrangement is in his best interests. Personnel can select the best qualified persons through testing and interviewing progams. This procedure saves the foreman time to concentrate on his production responsibilities. Top management approves with secret satisfaction, since the foreman can no longer pad the payroll with his own favorites. There was a time when a foreman could recruit a work force composed of sons, immediate relatives, and neighborhood friends. In this manner he built a personal loyalty which was not always in management's interest.

What was done with employment was subsequently done with every other personnel function of the foreman such as placement, training, transferring, making merit increases, and firing. In some cases the foreman could recommend and his word might carry weight. In other cases, like training, he might find

[5] Testimony of F.W. Taylor before Special Committee of the House of Representatives in 1912 to investigate Taylor and other systems of shop management.

his function removed by the establishment of a plant training school operated by the personnel department. He was told that all these things were done to help him. To the engineering helpers was added the corps of personnel helpers. Perhaps what hurt most was the new edict that he could recommend firing from his department but not from the company. One foreman described his reaction to this loss of function as follows:

I had this troublemaker. He was a solid gold bricker. He couldn't cut the buck on any job. I tried everything but he was lazy and he was a loudmouth. I caught him in the toilet after being away from his machine for over an hour. I told him he was through and to go upstairs and pick up his check. And damn, do you know what those college boys up in personnel did? He gives them some bull about being sick and weakly and the next day he is sitting at a bench in the department next to mine. He says to me, "Well, wise guy, you don't count for nothin' around here. Every time I see you I'm going to call you Mr. Nothin'."

If the foreman complained to personnel he was told that new facts were brought to light by the "exit interview" and that improvement in personnel relations necessitated more foreman training. Personnel was already planning a new course especially for foremen, and management was behind it one hundred per cent. To most foremen, this was the signal that they were in for another stretch in the charm school where they would be taught to be kind to their employees.

ORGANIZATIONAL-SYSTEMS ACCOMMODATION

Organizational systems are the procedures and techniques worked out by such departments as production planning and control, quality control, finance and accounting, organizational planning, and others. These departments all have their eyes on the plant floor where the money is made. Almost all changes proposed by management and staffs are aimed at the foreman and his workers, threatening the security or status of the foreman. The systems departments pose some of the greatest threats. Out of them pour new ideas and new production scheduling techniques. The existence of such systems not only demanded of the foreman an accommodation to the changes required but also required him to act as a buffer between the staff personnel and the workers. Men in white collars started filtering through the shop and often badgered employees. First it was an inspector; then an expediter; after that it was men or women from any of the above departments. Sometimes counselors from the personnel department came around and asked if there were any problems that anyone had. The foreman could claim that all of these intrusions were making it difficult to meet production quotas but the "helpers" kept coming and he was forced to live with them. Paperwork became so heavy that the foreman began to complain that he couldn't get out on the floor. Clerks were assigned to him but the management controls mounted. Management controls came to be regarded as a fundamental process in management. The foreman became involved in such control mechanisms as

> control over organization policies,
> control over rate of production,
> control over inventory,
> control over job specifications,
> control over planning,
> control over quality of production,
> control over product specifications,
> control over wages and salaries,
> control over costs,
> control over manpower,
> control over production methods,
> control over expenditures,
> control over public relations,
> control over supervisory time.

He might take solace in the fact that everyone in management was getting much of this same treatment. But he was expected to get out production, spend time in contact with his people, and still make out reports with strict punctuality. A small fragment of one day's activity for a foreman in an assembly department is described as follows:

The foreman was hurrying between two of the dozen workbenches in his department when the head of the plant maintenance department stopped him and thrust a jig into his hands.

Foreman: Is this done?

Maintenance man: What are we supposed to do with it?

Foreman: We want a plastic base on that to insulate it.

Maintenance man: We don't need the whole jig. Just give us the spec- ifications.

Foreman: And we need two more made up like that.

Maintenance man: (taking back the jig). Why didn't you say so? We will have to copy it. Do you have any pointers?

The foreman went to a nearby cabinet and looked through some boxes. While he was looking, the maintenance man was paged on the plant-wide call system. The maintenance man was phoning nearby when the foreman turned around. A product engineer joined the fore- man and began talking earnestly. The maintenance man hung up the phone and waited impatiently for the engineer to finish. They started a three-way discussion. Another engineer from the experimental section called the foreman away to get some partly finished instruments. The maintenance man left; the first engineer waited impatiently. Before the foreman could get the requested instruments, an employee stopped him to ask about some paperwork. An industrial engineer joined the product engineer and they talked briefly until the foreman returned. The experimental section engineer left, and the remaining two men turned to ask the foreman a series of technical questions. A girl from the production line called him away to answer another question and a foreman from another department came up to ask him for personnel to do some special packing.[6]

Note how the foreman has become exposed to strong pres- sures from several directions, and how each pressure affects his

---

[6] David N. Ulrich, Donald R. Booz, and Paul R. Lawrence, *Man- agement Behavior and Foreman Attitude* (Cambridge, Mass.: Harvard Graduate School of Business Administration, 1950), pp. 30-31.

capacity to handle the others. The organizational systems bring a tangle of interacting events with the foreman in the middle.

LABOR-RELATIONS ACCOMMODATION

The labor-relations accommodation came last and perhaps cut more heavily into the foreman's sense of independence than any one of the others. It was bad enough when the pressures were all management pressures from outside the department. Many foremen learned how to weaken and sometimes even nullify these pressures upon them. Unionization, however, meant that pressures from his subordinates were added. These came from stewards permanently stationed in his department. The elected steward would receive the greatest seniority and an opportunity to move freely among the workers soliciting grievances and complaints. These grievances and complaints represented potential trouble from higher management or higher union officials. Management's labor-relations head usually warned foremen of dire consequences which might come from the most innocent actions.

Be careful what you say to a worker or the NLRB may get you for prejudicial remarks about unionization.

Be careful what you do in firing a worker or the arbitrator will rule against you.

Be careful on how you assign overtime or the steward will catch you on the seniority clause

Be careful on your transfers. The contract is strict on the proper procedure and pay

Just be careful—you could cause a strike by worsening our labor relations.

In fact, if there is the slightest doubt in your mind, let us handle the problem.

The labor-relations climate can produce a work atmosphere full of foreboding and conspiratorial secrecy. The foreman is told to watch his lead men. "They are not in management and you can't trust them. They will be carrying anything they can find out into the union hall."

The steward is told to read his contract forward and backward and not let the foreman get away with anything. A steward relates how a foreman is dependent on the workers and the process they use to intimidate him:

A short time ago we had a lot of trouble with a certain foreman. He was an ex-committeeman by the way. He started out all right, was a good boy, but the guys took advantage of him. So he had to get back at them. He was making them toe the line . . . no quitting early, work from whistle to whistle, no setting down, no horseplay, this and that. I told the committeeman there, "You do the same thing. Every time he does any work, even if he picks up a box, write a grievance, violation of paragraph 66, violation of paragraph 32, violation of paragraph so and so." The first thing you know grievances started mounting—finally had a pile like that.

Things got so bad that they called a meeting of the top committee. I told them that the guys naturally jump at a foreman when he gets that way. This foreman was removed from that department. He was moved to our department and it's his last chance. If he doesn't make good in this department out he goes. So I went to the guy and told him, "It's your last chance here and you know it. You cooperate with us and we'll cooperate with you. If you don't we'll put the screws on you and out you go." Things are working out pretty good so far.[7]

The attitude of the foreman toward the union may be hostile or friendly, depending on his past experiences with it. If he has been a union man, he may not resent union restrictions on his activities. If he considers his job a step up the management ladder, he may resent the union's restrictions. In any case, it is another organization which limits his freedom of action.

THE FOREMAN'S DILEMMA

These accommodations required of foremen represent historic changes in role demands. The foreman of today, in contrast with his predecessors, has lost functions in the engineering, person-

---

[7] Delbert C. Miller and William H. Form, *Industrial Sociology*, rev. ed. (New York: Harper & Row, 1963), pp. 401-402.

nel, and organizational areas of his concern. But with every loss
in function he has acquired new obligations. He must know
more about production, personnel, engineering, organizational
procedures, and labor relations. His obligations have increased,
his authority has diminished. He lives poised between the two
worlds of management and labor. Donald Wray called the foremen the "marginal men of industry."[8] Fritz Roethlisberger called
them "masters and victims of double talk."[9]

The foreman's work position is the only one in the entire
structure that daily deals with *both* management and labor
firsthand. His *difficulties arise not so much out of lack of authority as out of the relative impossibility of reconciling two rather
incompatible ideologies or systems of sentiment.* Such a sharp
cleavage does not appear among the upper levels because there
is essential ideological agreement *within the management* hierarchy.

Management and worker ideologies whipsaw the foreman.
The foreman's boss and all levels above him are imbued with
the "logic of cost and effiicency." That is, their concern is to make
profit by applying rational, economic principles to production.
Consequently , they view the work plant as an impersonal economic machine which makes money. The workers are also units
to be considered in this process of moneymaking. Although managers do not regard relations among themselves impersonally,
they do think of problems on the plant floor as impersonal, finan-
cial ones.

The foreman's boss, the superintendent, has assimilated
this ideology of cost and efficiency, and tries to imbue it in his
foreman. The latter, however, have to deal with workers who
usually do not share management's conception of their role as
cost items. Workers do not consider themselves as machines to

[8] Donald E. Wray, "Marginal Men of Industry: The Foremen,"
American Journal of Sociology, 54:298-301 (January, 1949).
[9] Fritz J. Roethlisberger, "The Foreman: Master and Victim of
Double Talk," *Harvard Business Review,* Spring, 1945.

be moved about and used according to the best logic of efficiency. They have emotional stakes in their work and want to be considered accordingly. Management is sometimes aware of this fact on its own level but often is not so on the worker's level. The superintendent's view of the men below the foremen is impersonal.

The foreman, like any worker in the structure, does not want to incur the disapproval of his boss openly by violating norms of efficient economic behavior. Yet he must deal with the workers as people. He must meet situations which clear economic thinking cannot predict. He knows that he cannot disregard workers' sentiments about jobs, rates, profits, and procedures. He knows "it is impossible to uphold strictly the logic of efficiency without sometimes demoralizing the group." If he informs the superintendent of all the workers' resentments to management ideology, his boss will berate him for having so much dissension in his section. If he does not report these matters, his boss discovers them through other channels. Either alternative is dangerous.

THE FIRST-LINE SUPERVISOR AS A GENERAL TYPE

The discussion has centered around the foreman in production operations but the inference has been made that the internal-organization forces now bearing upon the foreman are impinging on all supervisors in commercial, governmental, and educational institutions. The first-line supervisor can thus be considered a general type and the foreman's position as in the cultural lead. It may be hypothesized that any variations from this lead type are due solely to time lags in the historic process of organizational change. Meanwhile, variations in organizational size, structure, technology, and the like create temporary differences. We know now that technology knows no bounds and that mass production has techniques for organizing men as well as for producing goods and devices.[10] Neither technology nor mass

[10] See Peter F. Drucker, *The New Society* (New York: Harper and Brothers, 1949).

production is any respecter of any institution, whether it be family, school, church, or traditional supervision pattern.

Elton Mayo pointed out that all supervisors and managers share three major functions. These are the technical, administrative, and human-relations functions. Floyd Mann and his associates have sought to get research evaluations of foremen and office supervisors, their central concern being with the technical, administrative, and human-relations functions of supervisors.[11] In the past five decades most attention has been directed toward the administrative and human-relations functions. A higher educational level is being demanded in supervisory posts. Some companies insist on the college graduate for the foreman's position and pay salaries between $8,000-$12,000. It has been suggested that most supervisors, when they can shift their attention from the pressure of immediate assignments, hold the following human-relations goals:

1. To raise the level of human motivation
2. To increase the readiness of subordinates to accept change
3. To improve the quality of all decisions
4. To develop teamwork and morale
5. To further the individual development of employees.[12]

All supervisors are being "helped" today in the pursuit of their tasks—personnel departments help screen some of the applicants, training departments attempt to provide training on the administrative and human-relations functions, staff experts help explain the new machines and equipment from computers to visual aids. Special functionaries worry about organizational

---

[11] Floyd C. Mann and L. Richard Hoffman, *Automation and the Worker* (New York: Henry Holt and Company, 1960). See especially Professor Mann's Chapter 3 in this present volume.

[12] Robert Tannenbaum, Irving R. Weschler, and Fred Massarik, *Leadership and Organization* (New York: McGraw-Hill Book Co. 1961), p. 78.

effectiveness and the test specialists devise measurement techniques. Morale surveys, supervisory reviews, and exit interviewing are common techniques in large organizations.

The lines of command grow longer and supervisors find themselves ever further alienated by communication and authority differentials between the top and the bottom rungs of management. No one is quite sure whether the supervisor is doing the job he should be doing. His paperwork is increasing but almost everyone is agreed that it should be reduced. His conference time is increasing but it is agreed that he should have more direct individual contact with members of his department. He is expected to get around more and find out what other departments are doing but he can't get away from his desk because of the pressure of reports. Top management can't understand why is he unable to report more quickly and his subordinates think he is spending too much time on desk work.

Max Weber's and Parkinson's predictions are coming to fruition. Weber predicted that as an organization grew in size it would engage in a growing number of technical specialists who would set an increasing number of controls in motion. Parkinson claimed that administrative staff growth would surpass the rate of growth in production personnel. These two forces of growth threaten the first-line supervisor with ever more controls and more reports. He becomes more of a manager than a supervisor and in some organizations like International Business Machines he is called a manager.

ORGANIZATIONAL ENVIRONMENT FACTORS INDUCING VARIATIONS IN ROLE DEMANDS

ORGANIZATIONAL SIZE

Sears, Roebuck and Company has conducted morale surveys regularly over more than 12 years. During that period the surveys have covered more than 100,000 employees working in several hundred different company units. The types of employees include sales, clerical, manual, professional, supervisory, and executive personnel. The units have ranged from fewer than 25 employees to more than 10,000. Worthy reports that mere size is unquestionably one of the most important factors in determining the quality of employee relationships: the smaller the unit the higher the morale and vice versa.[13]

The smaller organization represents a simpler social system than does the larger unit. There are fewer people, fewer levels in the organizational hierarchy, and a less minute subdivision of labor. The work of the employee becomes more meaningful to him and to his associates because all can see the relationship of work to the organization as a whole. A supervisor can maintain good employee contact in an easy face-to-face relationship. Work tasks can be enlarged and rotated to provide more interest. The supervisor escapes some of the controls which he might experience in a larger unit. He can settle grievances or get instructions easily from a boss who is accessible and who can make a decision without further reference to authority up the line.

Whyte has traced the impact of size on the organizational structure of the restaurant. He points out that each new level of supervision which is raised over the first-line supervisors in the kitchen or in the dining room brings new communication problems. The higher levels carry higher status, and social distance grows. Misunderstandings grow, status jealousies and rivalries emerge, and integration and control become more impersonal and authoritarian.[14]

In a study of a branch plant of a large organization with headquarters in New York, the communication problems between management and its supervisors were clearly revealed.[15] Between the management team and the direct-labor operators

[13] James C. Worthy, "Organizational Structure and Employee Morale," *American Sociological Review*, 15:170 (April, 1950).

[14] William F. Whyte, *Human Relations in the Restaurant Industry* (New York: McGraw-Hill Book Co., 1948).

[15] Ulrich, Booz, and Lawrence, *op. cit.* in note 6.

was a thin bridge of supervisors, foremen, and staff specialists. The operators worked on product lines which were continually being revised according to the dictates of the engineering department as interpreted by the foreman. Preoccupied with the demands made upon them by the hourly employees and staff specialists, the supervisory personnel felt they did not themselves have adequate capacity to deal with these demands. Yet their efforts to get the help they needed from general management were not successful. Instead, "management" made the strongest demands of all. The New York office required performance reports from supervisors, which were reviewed with reminders that their standing was important to their future career. In fact, supervisors became more preoccupied with what New York might think than what the general manager's evaluation might be. In an assembly department, the foreman formed the main link between the higher members of management and the hourly employees. Since a distinct gap existed between management and the employees, and since each group frequently misunderstood the other and often tried to put pressure on the other, the foreman was caught squarely between these opposing pressures. Daily he faced confusion, doubt, and conflict in trying to reconcile them.

The employees viewed the foreman as an instrument of management. But in the foreman's opinion, the superintendent entered the department only to criticize such matters as the way the floor had been swept. The foreman wished to see as little as possible of "His Majesty" and receive as few instructions from him as possible. The foreman felt the injustice of being held solely responsible for the correlation of all requirements set up by staff personnel as well as line superiors.

This case of the foreman caught in the middle becomes increasingly common with the growth of large scale absentee-owned enterprise. A self-perpetuating gap in communication between top management and subordinate personnel is a characteristic feature of many large organizations.

ORGANIZATIONAL STRUCTURE

Many structural variables can alter the status and role relationships of the supervisor and consequently his behavior toward his subordinates, his peers, and his superiors. The pertinent variables include: centralization vs. decentralization of the structure; authoritarian vs. democratic management; high managerial pressure vs. low pressure; presence of a strong, militant union vs. a weak, supine employee organization.

Centralization vs. Decentralization

In the more centralized complex organization, the individual supervisor or executive is subject to constant control and direction and has little opportunity to develop qualities of initiative and self reliance. Under extensive management decentralization, more reliance is placed on the personal initiative and capacity of the people in the organization. Supervisors enjoy considerable freedom in the way they accomplish their jobs. An organization with few layers of management and a minimum of formal controls places a premium on ability to stimulate and lead. Communication lines are shorter and the channels may allow freer communication both up and down the line. Worthy has concluded that "over-complexity of organizational structure is one of the most important and fundamental causes of poor management-employee relationships and until this problem is faced and corrected no substantial improvement in these relationships is likely to be possible."[16] Sears, Roebuck and Company, General Motors, and International Business Machines are three organizations which have simplified their organizational structure by cutting away levels of management or by decentralization of operations into autonomous divisions.

International Business Machines adopted a policy calling for only three levels of management in the factory, expressed

---

[16] Worthy, *op. cit.* in note 13, p. 174.

as management, manager and men.[17] (Manager refers here to the foreman position.) In 1940 there were six levels of authority in the main manufacturing departments. They were: executive assistant, superintendent and assistant superintendent, department supervisor, foreman, assistant foreman and key men, operator. By 1947, the assistant foreman and key men had been dropped and the superintendent became plant head in charge of all manufacturing. This cut the number of levels from six to four. The key men were eliminated and the foreman became the sole supervisor in every section. The number of workers per foreman, instead of remaining constant or increasing, fell during the years that the company doubled in size. This change was accomplished by splitting sections and increasing the number of "managers" and clerks. Meanwhile the foreman's job was enlarged. He was, as far as possible, to manage all the affairs of his own section— technical, administrative, and human relations. The company defined his functions as employing, training, supervising, promoting, and discharging. Such of these powers that had been exercised by the personnel department were transferred to the line supervisors.

Many effects could be traced to the changes. Contacts increased between workers and their foremen with workers initiating proportionately more contacts. During contacts, workers talked proportionately longer and foremen more completely processed the complaints of their workers. The number and quality of contacts between foremen and management also changed in a comparable way.

Sears, Roebuck and Company, and General Motors have both made changes toward decentralization to give more authority to the operating branch or unit.[18] General Motors has put

[17] F. L. W. Richardson, Jr., and Charles R. Walker, *Human Relations in an Expanding Company* (New Haven: Yale University Labor and Management Center, 1938), pp. 14-31.

[18] Peter F. Drucker, *Concept of the Corporation* (New York: John Day Company, 1946), pp. 65-66.

its Chevrolet, Buick, Oldsmobile, Pontiac, Cadillac, and General Motors Truck under autonomous direction, with central administration confined to regulation and advice. Two objective yardsticks have been set up to measure the relative efficiency of the divisions: (1) base pricing, which gives an objective measure of the efficiency of the corporation and of its subdivisions as a producer; (2) competitive market standing, which shows automatically and immediately the efficiency of the corporation as a seller. Together these two gauges are supposed to show overall efficiency and supply an immediate and objective check on decisions and policies. The objective yardstick of base pricing and cost analysis is applied to the individual foreman as well. Each year the foremen make an efficiency budget of costs and output for their departments which focuses on three main criteria of productive efficiency: output per man hour, output per dollar of wages, output per dollar invested in machines. The budget, and the extent to which a foreman lives up to it, expresses the foreman's abilities both as a leader of men and as a technically competent person. Shortcomings in either capacity will at once become manifest. Both the foreman and management are given an objective, though incomplete, yardstick for the determination of a foreman's abilities as a supervisor. In implementing the autonomous plant policy definite attempts were made to test promising foremen and train them for more responsible jobs. In several divisions the foremen were brought into the councils of management, although usually in an advisory capacity. The meetings, seldom formal, were regarded by both management and the foremen as the best means, next to the yardstick of cost analysis, to arrive at a fair basis for selection and promotion.[19]

Authoritarian vs. Democratic Management

Kurt Lewin and Ronald Lippitt have shown in their classic studies of social climate that leadership behavior of an authoritarian, democratic, or laissez-faire type has distinct conse-

---

[19] *Ibid.*, pp. 165-167.

quences for the behavior of group members. Mann, Likert, Pelz, and others have shown that each subordinate leader is influenced profoundly by the behavior of his superior. The supervisor's emphasis on production-centered or employee-centered practices can be directly traced to the orientations of the superior. Mann and Dent have shown that a supervisor rated highly both by his superiors and by his employees more often says:

> His superior lets him participate in decision making.
> His superior lets him know what he thinks of his work.
> His superior frequently asks him for his opinion.[20]

Pelz discovered a linking-pin function. Briefly, this function refers to the relationship which reaches from the leader downward to his subordinates and upward to the superior. If a supervisor has above-average influence or power with his own bosses and he follows procedures which are generally good supervisory behavior, his subordinates tend to react favorably. However, if supervisors are below average in the amount of influence they have with their superiors, they usually fail to obtain favorable reactions and often secure adverse reactions although they practice the same desirable supervisory practices. These findings have been interpreted to show that the supervisor, to function effectively, must have sufficient influence with his own superior to be able to affect the superior's decisions when required.[21]

High Managerial Pressure vs. Low Pressure

Argyris has studied two similar plants in which considerable managerial pressure was applied.[22] The foremen said that in

---

[20] Floyd C. Mann and James K. Dent, *Appraisals of Supervisors and Attitudes of their Employees in an Electric Power Company* (Ann Arbor: University of Michigan Institute for Social Research, 1954).

[21] Rensis Likert, *New Patterns of Management* (New York: McGraw-Hill Book Co., 1961), pp. 5-25.

[22] Chris Argyris, *Understanding Organizational Behavior* (Homewood, Ill.: Dorsey Press, 1960).

order to be effective they must strive hard (1) to keep everyone busy with work, (2) to guarantee a fair take-home pay, (3) to distribute the easy and tough jobs fairly, and (4) to leave the employees alone as much as possible. To do all these, a successful foreman develops a passive leadership style, cultivating neither direct nor human-relations skills. The passive leadership style involves acceptance of a "psychological contract" with employees (what Alvin Gouldner called the "indulgency pattern"). The employees maintain high production, low grievances, and the like if the foreman guarantees and respects the norms of the employee informal culture (that is, lets the employees alone, makes certain they make adequate wages, and have secure jobs). The impact of the psychological contract is to simplify the foreman's job. Thus 65 per cent described themselves by saying, "I have nothing to offer except the technical abilities I learned on my job"; and "I do not have any abilities; there's not much to me."[23] Such leaders do not tend to possess the active, striving characteristics desired by management.

Management consistently put pressure on the foreman to break the pattern just described. The foremen expressed high dissatisfaction with this pressure from management and complained also of low status on the job, undercutting of their authority, low wages in relation to employees' wages, and lack of any policy-making role in their own department. The dissatisfaction of the foremen only brought further pressure from management, and a self-maintaining feedback process was established.

Nothing was done to get at the root of the problem—namely, the reconstruction of the formal requirements of the jobs to provide more challenging motivation from both employees and foremen. Instead, a budget system was introduced to control costs more rigorously. Budgets (1) apply never-ending pressure, (2) constantly raise production goals, (3) increasingly tighten piece-rate systems, (4) strive to eliminate informal activities such as the employees' work kitty, (5) place line people

---

[23] *Ibid.*, pp. 96-97.

in positions where they cannot build employee morale, (6) lead to interpersonal hostilities among managerial personnel.[24] Foremen were being put under high pressure and they feared what would happen if employees saw budgets as pressure devices. One foreman said:

Jessuz, I can't use these goddam things as the bright boys upstairs think they can be used. Why if I take one of these damn things to the boys in Department A, most of whom have been in this company over ten years, they'd tell me to shove them.[25]

The top budget people expressed disgust with the foremen for their unwillingness to use the budget system. They felt that the problem was one of educating the foremen, whom they perceived as "not so bright." One budget man said, "Someday someone is going to have a light a firecracker under somebody's rear. All we hear is excuses and all we get are delays." The foremen counteracted with silence, careful digs at the budget system, and excuses.[26]

TECHNOLOGY

Technology is an important environmental factor affecting the supervisor and those employees under his supervision. Increased mechanization exemplified by assembly line production has had the effect of reducing the skill level of workers as well as their discretion.[27] Skilled craftsmen have been replaced by semiskilled operators. Jobs have become repetitive and mechanically paced, and require only minimal abilities. The worker has fewer opportunities for interpersonal contacts; he feels his chances for promotion are slim, and he feels bound to the line which demands a strict conformance to schedule.

---

[24] Chris Argyris, Chapter 5 in Mason Haire (ed.), *Modern Organization Theory* (New York: John Wiley and Sons, 1959), p. 150.

[25] *Ibid.*, p. 151.

[26] *Ibid.*, p. 151.

[27] W. Lloyd Warner and J. O. Low, *The Social System of the Modern Factory* (New Haven: Yale University Press, 1947), pp. 66-89.

What is the impact upon the foreman? To deal with all these elements in the work environment, the foreman must provide as many counter influences as he can. He must mediate between the rigidities and impersonalities of higher management and the personal needs of the workers.[28] The assembly line itself makes an endless variety of demands. In fact, the typical foreman is engaged in some four to six hundred separate episodes in the course of his working day.[29] The conveyor keeps the foreman moving rapidly from place to place and doing many different things. While the worker is experiencing excessive repetitiveness, the foreman is experiencing excessive discontinuity. Obviously, nearly all supervisory and executive jobs are characterized by some degree of discontinuity and by the pressure of unanticipated interruptions. The foreman, like any good executive, needs the ability to hold simultaneously in mind details of many uncompleted actions so that later at the appropriate moment he may close the episode. In short, two major demands are made upon the foreman of an assembly line. He must (1) provide skills which enable him to counterbalance anonymity with a personal relationship, and (2) withstand interruptions with a minimum of frustration.

Further mechanization of technical processes, particularly automation, has been expected to raise the level of skill and responsibility of operators, to release the more skilled worker from close supervision, and to provide a wider range of discretionary freedom over his actions. Studies of automated factories do not bear out these expectations.[30] The conclusion that emerges from these studies on the social consequences of automation is that as long as automation is not accompanied by a higher level

---

[28] Charles R. Walker, *et. al.*, *The Foreman on the Assembly Line* (Cambridge, Mass.: Harvard University Press, 1956).

[29] *Ibid.*, p. 124-125.

[30] William A. Faunce, "Automation in the Automobile Industry," *American Sociological Review*, 23:401-407 (1958); Charles R. Walker, *Toward the Automatic Factory* (New Haven: Yale University Press, 1957); Richard L. Simpson, "Vertical and Horizontal Communication

of worker skill, it does not result in increased discretion. Job satisfaction may not be notably improved and may in fact be reduced. Given a low level of skill of operators, the more complex machines may require closer supervision and greater centralization of decision making. In the comparative study of an older power plant with a newly automated power plant in the same company, Mann and Hoffman concluded that . . .

. . . it appears that since the automated production process is self-regulating under normal circumstances, employees have more time to be concerned with their own needs and the supervisor must therefore be even more concerned with and skillful at the interpersonal aspects of his job. Our data suggest that since the technical complexities of automation may be handled adequately by the non-supervisory operating force, the supervisor's job will be to concentrate more on the direction of employee activities and the meeting of their needs."[31]

The impact of mechanization and specialization in work organizations seems to point toward similar demands on first-line supervisors. They must have interpersonal skills to provide a counterweight to the impersonal forces of larger size, centralization of decision making, and the isolation which can accompany the specialist as he is drawn into his own "narrower" communication channel. Supervisors must act as buffers between their employees and the "outside world." They must mediate conflicts and interpret their own departmental activities. Their tolerance level must be high to endure frustrations and conflicts. Their own technical skills become less important and have meaning only as they provide guides for recruitment and placement, and stimulate insights into personal needs of their individual employees and the aspirations of the group.

---

in Formal Organizations," *Administrative Science Quarterly*, 4:188-196 (1959); Floyd C. Mann and Lawrence K. Williams, "Observations on the Dynamics of a Change to Electronic Data Processing Equipment," *Administrative Science Quarterly*, 5:217-256 (1960).

[31] Floyd C. Mann and L. Richard Hoffman, *Automation and the Worker* (New York: Holt, Rinehart and Winston, 1960), p. 209.

AUTHORITY OF THE SUPERVISOR

It has been shown that the supervisor must make accommodations to historic changes in the general definition of his role and also to specific factors which may be present in his particular work environment. A central thread runs through all of these factors and that is the supervisor's authority. The difference between line and staff is disappearing.[32] The supervisor, whether a line officer or a staff officer, increasingly gains his authority by the use of influence and persuasion and his force comes from an expertise based on an understanding of the cooperative process which he is trying to direct. The erosion of line authority as the only authority system has occurred because of two changes. The first has been the democratization of the labor force buttressed by changing economic and social ideals and reinforced by labor organizations. The second has been the growth in importance of staff functions. Haire quotes an executive who said, "Such and such a department used to be staff, but it has become so important that it's now a line function.[33] In many organizations marketing has been the first department to be officially recognized as coequal with production, but in actual practice most staff functions have been accorded unofficial authority. If a staff is to accept responsibility for its functions it must also have authority. It has steadily gained that authority by the necessity which gives rise to its functions. Sales, labor relations, engineering, finance, personnel, and public relations have all won their place as sources of expertise basic to the functioning of the line and to the total enterprise. The line supervisor has become more and more like a staff supervisor because as internal differences in the importance of functions diminished the same sociocultural environment dominated. Collaborative effort now has a common denominator—all supervisors must become competent in the technical, ad-

---

[32] Mason Haire (ed.), *Organization Theory in Industrial Practice* (New York: John Wiley and Sons, 1962), pp. 4-6.

[33] *Ibid.*, p. 5.

ministrative, and human-relations responsibilities and play roles in close cooperative relations with those functionaries with whom their responsibilities intertwine.

FOUR TYPES OF SUPERVISORY BEHAVIOR

Under the new demands of his complicated organizational environment, there seem to be four ways for the supervisor to work out his difficult role. Each has it own stresses and strains.[34]

1. A supervisor may view his role as *management's representative*. The supervisor may easily become the authoritarian, task-oriented supervisor who puts management's goals first and the employees' needs second. In this situation, not only may alienation and unionization be higher, but the employees will follow their own informal leaders.

2. The second type of supervisor identifies strongly with the *employees*. His first loyalty is to them and in his communication with management he will tend to play up employee demands and the difficulties in executing certain tasks and orders. He can easily become indulgent about meeting production goals.[35] He may thus win employee acceptance but alienate management, which may not trust him with the result that his influence with his supervisors is greatly weakened. He may not get what he wants and indeed he is likely to get pressure from above to tighten up his department. If he tries to put pressure on the employees they resent his violation of habitual standards. They may become confused as to what kind of person he really is and he is caught between ambivalent role conceptions of himself.

3. A third type of supervisor tries to keep both management and his employees happy and he is trapped in a dilemma of *dual loyalty*. To management he promises high performance

---

[34] Amitai Etzioni, "Human Relations and the Foreman," *Pacific Sociological Review*, 1:33-38, (Spring, 1958).

[35] Alvin W. Gouldner, *Wildcat Strike* (Yellow Springs, Ohio: The Antioch Press, 1954); see his description of the "indulgency pattern," p. 19. Chris Argyris, *Understanding Organizational Behavior* (Homewood, Ill.: Dorsey Press, 1960), p. 96.

and puts the blame on employees for failure to keep his promises; to the employees he conveys loyalty and understanding and blames management for any of their needs which he has not fulfilled. He is an expert at double talk and dissembling behavior. If the employees or management become aware of this kind of gamesmanship the supervisor may lose the confidence of both parties.

4. The fourth type is the supervisor who is oriented toward other supervisors as a social group. This supervisor will seek association with other supervisors in an effort to protect his own rights, privileges, and authority. He will try to be fair to both management and employees but will try to keep the interest of his own group in mind. Such orientations have sometimes led to the formation of formal associations with and without the blessing of management. Since the Taft-Hartley Act excluded supervisors from union coverage, supervisors have no recourse except to form their own associations. In many cases, management has led the way in sponsoring supervisors' associations in order to identify the first-line supervisor as a management representative. The identification with management is the goal desired by the sponsor but identification with supervision may result, with repercussions of the kind associated with the supervisor attempting to maintain dual loyalty.

The supervisor may find himself playing all of these different roles on different occasions. He is not cast in a stable role situation, yet all of the forces tend to pull him into the position where he must learn to acquire dual loyalty and appropriate behavior. Mann and Dent have shown that when supervisors are regarded by their employees as pulling for both the company and the employees they rate high in both the employees' regard and the management's regard. At least, that is the way it works out in the accounting division of the Detroit Edison Company.[36]

In the long run, all managerial leaders must accept the fact

[36] Floyd C. Mann and James K. Dent, *Appraisals of Supervisors and Attitudes of Their Employees in an Electric Power Company* (Ann Arbor: University of Michigan Institute for Social Research, 1954).

that they must reconcile conflicting interests and needs. The skill with which they do it is a precious talent requiring continuous learning and experience. The characteristics of honesty, patience, and integrity are integral to the highest performance capabilities. Thus, the successful supervisor has evolved from the authoritarian Bull of the Woods to the persuasive, mediating leader. He is better educated, better paid, and more skilled in interpersonal relations than ever before in history. In his position he has added empathy and social insight to what was once only naked authority and technical ability.

Index of Topics

133

Index of Names

137